MOMENTS LOST
A MEMOIR

Moments Lost

A Memoir

WAVEY HULL

LUMINARE PRESS

WWW.LUMINAREPRESS.COM

Luminare Press
442 Charnelton St.
Eugene, OR 97401
www.luminarepress.com

LCCN: 2022902172
ISBN: 978-1-64388-879-8

To

Mommy and Junior

AUTHOR'S NOTE

This story includes events as described to the author by the people in the story, as well as the author's firsthand knowledge. Some names and other incidental details have been changed to protect their privacy.

INTRODUCTION

I was not there. My brother, Robert aka *Junior*, named after my father, and me, named after my mother, Wendy, grew up and left the instant we were old enough, leaving Mommy behind to face our father alone. I knew the sound and the terror of his black Marlin 35 rifle with its pistol grip from the day he caught a man siphoning gas from Mommy's Monte Carlo. I knew the fear Mommy felt as she backed down the driveway, the first shot just skimming the top of the gray roof of her two-door 1982 Buick Riviera. I had seen the whole scene—or something like it—a hundred times before.

CHAPTER 1

The Chase

Bam! Where do you think you going, bitch? You won't leave me. I will kill you first!

Bam!

Not stopping to look both ways, Mommy frantically made a left turn out of the driveway and down Columbus Boulevard, headed for the Long Island Expressway. The gas gauge on the Buick Riviera read three-quarters full. She couldn't make it to Delaware, to Mom Mom's house. The next best bet was Aunt Gayle in Pennsylvania. Her house would be safe. She was tough and not afraid of my father, and that was why he hated her so. She was the one woman who did not take any shit off him. Plus, Uncle Tony was a policeman, and he would not hesitate to shoot to kill.

As Mommy sped down the road, she prayed out loud. "Lord, please make a way for me to get away from this man. Don't let him catch me. I want to live to see my babies again."

Beeeep! Beeeep! Beeeep!

He was tailgating her. She ducked her head close to the steering wheel. Did he have the gun with him? Would he take aim?

She sped through the second stoplight on Miller Avenue. Where were the Brentwood police when she needed them? She had to let someone know she was coming, but she was too afraid to stop. The 7-Eleven was a few miles away.

Maybe she could lose him in traffic and use the pay phone there. She had used that same phone many times before when she wanted to make a collect call to her mother in Laurel, Delaware. A call could not be made from the house without him listening on the line from the bedroom, thinking no one could hear him breathing heavily into the receiver—or maybe he wanted her to hear. He examined the monthly phone bill to confirm that she had not made any long-distance calls to her family.

She glanced in the mirror. He was gone. The last light must have caught him. She made a sharp left and raced to the 7-Eleven. A truck was parked in the lot, and she pulled up next to it, hoping to hide her car. She jumped out, realized she left her keys in the ignition, and ran back to retrieve them. She then scrambled for the phone booth, snatched the receiver, and firmly pressed 0 for operator.

"Operator, how may I help you?"

Mommy yelled frantically, "He shot after me, and now he is chasing me! I need to place a collect call! Hurry!"

"What is the number? What is the name of the party?'"

"3, 0, 2, 8, 3, 5, 4, 3, 3, 0, Ernest and Francine Hamilton."

"Your name is?"

"Wendy. Please hurry. This is an emergency." Her voice trembled.

"Connecting now. Please hold the line."

"Hamilton residence. How may I help ya?" Pop Pop's sharp, abrupt, direct tone always sounded as if you had reached a major corporation and the CEO happened to answer.

"This is the operator with a collect call from Wendy. Sir, will you accept?"

"Yes, I will."

"Daddy! Daddy! It's me," Mommy cried.

"Wendy! Wendy, I can hardly hear you! Hold on." He called out to Mom Mom. "Francie! Francie! Come get the phone. It's Wendy, and I can hardly hear her!"

"Daddy, hurry up!"

"Hello?" Mom Mom's steady, firm tone was reassuring.

"Mom, it's me!" Tears streamed down her high, chiseled cheekbones.

"I can hear you." Mom Mom spoke calmly and quickly. "What's the matter?" She moved her mouth away from the phone to direct Pop Pop. "Ernest, turn off the pot on the stove."

"Mom, he's got a gun! He's chasing me in the car!"

"Where are you? Do you have any money?"

"Mom, call Gayle and let her know I am heading that way. I am on the Jersey Turnpike. All I have is three-quarters' tank of gas, and I cannot stop anymore. I'm coming!"

"Good Lord, that's not enough, Wendy! Can you make your way to Ms. Spencer's house?"

"No, Mom. It's late, and I don't want to involve them. He shot after me twice already!"

"I'm calling Joe and Mike. They are not scared of that nigga. They will shoot his ass in a minute!" Joe and Mike were Mommy's brothers.

"Mom, I have to go! Call Gayle now!"

"What exit are you getting off—"

The dial tone was deafening in Mom Mom's ear as my Mother dropped the phone and ran for the car.

How absurd that this all began with a Whopper from Burger King.

The trouble that day began in Brentwood, Long Island, late 1980s, during the dinner hour. He always bragged about his Marlin 35 being the best rifle around with its pinpoint accuracy. It was that same precision that had shot a man in the ass who attempted to siphon gas from Mommy's two-door, burnt-orange Monte Carlo in the middle of the night during the 1979 gas strike. He often beat her or stomped her, but this time, his daily terror was taken to another level.

This night, she feared that accuracy as he tried to hit another moving target: her.

He had sent her to Burger King. Her mission was to go through the drive through for a fish sandwich and fries. When she got home and gave him the wrapped food, he ripped it open like a child opening a present on Christmas day. With his stubby, fat hands, he pulled out the sandwich and examined it carefully. The grease-stained bag contained a Whopper with cheese and cold fries.

"What the fuck is this shit?"

She turned around just in time to duck. The sandwich grazed the top of her head, shreds of lettuce landing in her hair. The fries scattered on the pristine, polished, walnut-stained floor.

"You dumb BITCH! Did you check the muthafuckin' bag before you drove off?"

Mommy's voice trembled. "No, I didn't. What is the matter, Robert?"

"I'll tell you what the fuck is the matter. You got the wrong muthafuckin' order!"

"Okay, I'll take it back." She shuddered as she walked backward out of the living room, her eyes fixed on him.

"Fuck it. Now the shit is all over the floor! What the fuck am I gonna eat?"

"I can get you some chicken."

"Did I say I wanted some muthafuckin' chicken? If I wanted some goddamn chicken, I would have sent you for some! You so muthafuckin' stupid, just like your fuckin' family!"

He leapt off the chair and came toward her. His walk was always with purpose. Upright and confident at five feet six, he had the presence of a giant when he entered any space. Oddly, his round belly was a sign of distinction to him, and he held it forward proudly as he advanced. The intimidating scowl he wore forewarned anyone that he was not to be played with. He was always a man about business. His business.

"Bitch, you better not be here when I get back!" Mercifully, he passed by her but stopped at the hall closet. That closet held only two things: coats and his Marlin 35. The rattling of the bullets in the box was warning enough.

Mommy grabbed her purse off the floor. Her hands shook with terror as she clawed through it for her car keys. The thundering of his stomping feet was drawing near. She ran desperately for the front door, her right hand turning the latch, pressing down on the lever, yanking the door handle—each act taking an eternity. She raced down the driveway and fell into the driver's seat, banging her leg against the doorframe as she slammed the door shut. She struggled to find the ignition in the dusk-lit sky and get the key in. His shouted threats brought no one from the upper middle-class neighborhood to her rescue.

Leaving the 7-Eleven in a panic, she raced the Riviera through the streets and merged onto the Long Island Expressway. Her eyes were deceiving her—this could not be, it just could not be. Headlights frantically wove from the middle lane to the fast lane. Horns honked behind her. How could he have found her? This could not be happening. Did he see her?

The tractor trailer in front of her would present excellent camouflage if she could get on the other side and into the slow lane. With the precision of an Indy racer, she veered the Riviera behind the truck and into the slow lane, keeping pace, being careful not to outrun it.

When would the gas run out? When would he realize that she was on the other side of the truck? Was he stupid enough to bring the gun with him? Where was a police car when she needed it?

She prayed, *Dear Lord, please do not let this man catch me. He wants to kill me, and you cannot let that happen. I have children to look after and a family that I love. Make a way, Lord, please make a way.*

Last time she made this journey, my brother and I were barely out of diapers.

The tangled route around New York City was challenging and packed with cars. She tried to recognize the exits, not sure which one led to the New Jersey Turnpike, and then to Pennsylvania and eventually to Gayle's house. The green-and-white highway sign read I-95 South Cross Bronx Expressway. Was that the right exit? She hoped something would trigger a distant memory to lead her in the right direction. At least she was able to maintain her speed, keeping pace with the tractor trailer.

The sudden blow of the trucker's horn made her jump. He was trying to cut her off. His right turn signal was on, his horn blasting. She slowed, fearing he would run her off the road. The trailer whipped in front of her with razor precision, and the trucker never lost speed. She blew her horn at him to signal that he was wrong in his aggression.

She looked left. His car was gone. He must have sped off straight ahead in hot pursuit in the fast lane, thinking she had continued ahead of him.

She looked ahead. The back of the tractor trailer in front of her had two words: Purdue Chicken. The Purdue

Chicken farms were in Maryland, which meant he had to pass through Pennsylvania to get there. Her keen instincts went into overdrive. *He knows what exit to take. I can follow him. Thank you, Jesus! The Lord works in mysterious ways.*

She followed the truck over the George Washington Bridge until she saw the signs to the New Jersey Turnpike. Now she knew where she was, but would she make it? Her bladder was not cooperating. It never did when Mommy was nervous, even though we were pros at holding our bladders for long periods of time. When we left home for long trips out of state, he refused to pull over at rest stops. He said we pulled over only when he was ready, which was rare. He was more concerned with "making time" and arriving at our destination under time. He used these achievements as conversation, boasting at how he sped to Maryland or Virginia or wherever in record time. Little did his audience know the suffering behind his showboating.

Mommy desperately needed to find a rest stop, but she flexed her thighs and picked up speed.

Had Mom Mom Hamilton called everybody? My Uncle Mike lived in North Jersey, ninety miles outside of New York City. Uncle Joe lived in Virginia, about ninety-five miles from Delaware, where Mom Mom and Pop Pop lived. Mommy hoped they had been called and hoped she wouldn't need them. One of the main reasons Mommy stayed with my father was to protect her family. She knew what he was capable of as evidenced by the brutal beatings we endured. He threatened many times that he would hurt Mom Mom, Pop Pop, and my uncles. He said my aunt needed someone to set her mouth straight once and for all since her husband could not do it. Mommy preferred to endure his thrashings if it remained in the house. Her grace, mercy, and forgiveness were her kryptonite, but this was an emergency. What would happen if they came? What would he do to them?

Uncle Mike was the nonviolent type. His round, tortoise-shell glasses made him look every bit like the oil executive that he was. Real estate investing was his love, and he owned several rental properties in the New Jersey and Philadelphia areas. He was five foot seven, slim, and always impeccably dressed in European-designed suits tailored to perfection. He paired his jackets and overcoats with precision to vintage, handmade, plaid cashmere scarves woven in deep mahogany, cabernet, or ebony. His perfectly shined leather wingtips were barely worn in. He always smelled nice.

Uncle Joe was the country boy. He was a schoolteacher by trade, but his love for the country landed him on a farm in Virginia. Brilliantly skilled with his hands, he built his two-story, four-bedroom, two-and-a-half-bath home from the ground up, complete with a black, nickel-plated antique wood burning stove. He raised pigs, chickens, and any other animal that generated hefty profits, and he managed several investment properties. His muscular, five-eleven frame was intimidating. His darker complexion mirrored Mom Mom's. A look of mischief was always on his face; whenever he entered a room, he was up to something, as Mom Mom would say, or was getting ready to get into something. Of Mom Mom's five children, he was one of the fighters. He fiercely protected his family, especially his sisters. If you messed with either of them, he was guaranteed to whoop your ass. He had studied karate and missed earning his black belt only because he had drawn blood on his opponent. Guns, aluminum bats, knives, and nun chucks were not unfamiliar territory. He couldn't wait for the day to render an ass whooping to Mommy's husband.

Mommy's nerves were getting the best of her, and her bladder could not hold out. She exited at the next rest stop, praying that he was not close behind. She found a corner of the parking lot that was masked by overflowing trees and parked. The smell of Arby's chicken reminded her that she had not eaten. She found the ladies room and splashed water on her face to stay alert. As the coarse, brown paper towel scratched lightly over her face, she thought of Mom Mom. Should she call again and tell her where she was? Was he waiting for her in the parking lot? It had been at least an hour since she saw those glaring headlights behind her, weaving in and out of traffic. She left the ladies' room, went to the nearby payphone inside the rest stop, and picked up the receiver.

"Wendy?"

"Daddy?" The sound of his voice was a relief.

"Ernest, where is she? Did she run out of gas? Ask her where she is," Mom Mom called in the background.

"I'm on the New Jersey Turnpike. I don't know where he is. I think I may have lost him."

"Ernest, hand me the phone," Mom Mom said.

"Mom, I had to stop to pee."

"That's all right, baby, that is all right. You could have peed in the car. We would have cleaned it up. Don't worry about a thing. Mike and Joe are on their way. I called Gayle, and Tony is on his way as well. Can you get somewhere and hide until they get there? I don't know which one will arrive first. Joe was two sheets in the wind when he said he was on his way from Virginia. That crazy fool has got his guns. Gayle said Tony has his piece strapped on that hip and one on his ankle. Tell me where you are so when they call back, I can let them know where to find you."

"Molly Pitcher. Exit eight."

"Find somewhere out of the way and wait. They're on their way."

The aroma from Arby's lingered in the air, but Mommy's nerves got the best of her. It was more important that she find a place to hide until help arrived. A family of four was leaving Arby's, so she walked fast to blend in with them and then into the night air. With her head down, she walked to the corner of the lot, unlocked her car door, and got in. A tractor trailer had pulled up beside her car while she was inside the rest area. It blocked her vision and made it hard for her to see out. Somehow, she knew her brothers would find her before he did.

The screech of tires woke her from her semiconscious state. She was too afraid to look. She scrunched down as far as she could as a car door slammed behind her and footsteps approached.

CHAPTER 2

The Encounter

Mommy fell in love with our father in college. He was a smooth talker, handsome, with a lighter-brown skin tone, and a football and track star. He would also fight at the drop of a dime—kick ass and take names. Mommy told us about how some guy was giving her the googly eyes, and my father walked up to the guy and started pummeling him. She tried to pull them apart, and he cursed her for involving herself in man's business. People had seen my father beat down grown men when he was in college, so few challenged him.

Our father's brother was not the fighting type. However, my Uncle Kenny used to tell us that if anyone bothered him at school, he would come home and tell his big brother, because he knew he and his gang of thugs would go to school the next day and take care of the bully. My Uncle Kenny told me that my father used to beat the bullies so bad that sometimes he was afraid to tell him when someone messed with him in school for fear of what he would do. One time, my father found out that Uncle Kenny had not told him someone was taking his lunch every day. My father beat the shit out of Uncle Kenny for not letting him know, went to school the next day, and beat the bully so bad that he broke his nose and disfigured his lip.

Women fell at the feet of the football and track star and hung on his every word with his sweet-talking ways. He reminded Mommy that she should consider herself lucky: he could have chosen anyone, and he chose her. The men wanted to be like him, and the women wanted him. It is a cliché that came true.

At their first meeting, he showed his charming, funny, intellectual, talkative side, which she later found was a veiled spell to gain her trust. She caught onto his cunning gamesmanship too late. Her love for him turned to fear due to the threats he made good on.

Mom Mom told me that she wished Mommy would have walked away from that devil when she was in college. Mom Mom said when she and Pop Pop got wind of him beating her, they pleaded with her to walk away. She did until he came to Mom Mom's house to woo her back, promising he would work to change and swearing on his mother's life. He described the brutal beatings as temper tantrums that could be corrected overnight. He blamed the stress of the world.

Mom Mom and Pop Pop knew better.

Once, when Robert and I were toddlers, Mommy went back to Mom Mom's house. He arrived shortly thereafter and swore he would never hit her again. Although my grandparents did not believe him, Mommy did, and that was all that mattered. As soon as he left Mom Mom's house in Laurel, Delaware, he beat her all the way back to his mother's house in Salisbury, Maryland, twenty-five miles away. He warned her that if she tried it again, he would kill her, her children, and her parents. Family was everything to Mommy, and she vowed, first and always, to protect her parents from harm.

Mom Mom and Pop Pop Hamilton were immensely proud people. They were forced out of elementary school to work on the farm to help support their families. When they met and married, Pop Pop worked as a butcher. He would come home after a full day of butchering and then tend to his stock of pigs and chickens and an acre of farmland.

Mom Mom did days work for affluent white families in Delaware while she and Pop Pop raised a family of five Christian children in the 1940s during segregation. Four of their children went to college and earned bachelor's or master's degrees. Another was a career military serviceman.

Mom Mom was the woman of the house—she managed the household budget, cooked, cleaned, and cared for the children and Pop Pop.

She saw to it that my aunts' and uncles' spiritual needs were met, talked to them about God, and lived a life of faith. She brought them to Sunday school every week to learn more about God and the Baptist faith while she attended the morning worship service.

Pop Pop did not attend service as frequently as Mom Mom, because oftentimes he stayed behind to tend to the family farm that produced chickens, pigs, collard greens, mustard greens, kale, winter cress, string beans, cabbage, corn, sweet potatoes, white potatoes, watermelons, cantaloupes, tomatoes, butterbeans, peas, cucumbers, and squash. Most of their meat was fresh from the pig pen or chicken coop.

Mom Mom rose early in the morning to prepare a breakfast of crispy scrapple, sage sausage or bacon, buttered grits, scrambled eggs, and homemade biscuits with canned strawberry preserves, marmalade, or grape jelly to slather between the hot biscuits. She sat a glass decanter of milk in the middle of the table. On those cold mornings, a big pot of oatmeal could be found warming on the stove. While the children ate, Mom Mom made lunches for them and Pop Pop and then got ready for work.

My father always said Pop Pop did not keep Mom Mom in her place, but we knew better. He was jealous of the love and support my mother's family had for one another, which was something he never had and could not bear for us to have. He said that Mom Mom was nosing around in our business and Pop Pop was weak.

We were not allowed to accept gifts from Mom Mom and Pop Pop. My father would intercept them, beat my mother for receiving them, and force us to watch as he broke them with his bare hands or stomped on them and threw them away, wrapping paper and all. Though she had only an elementary school education, Mom Mom was a wise woman and learned how to get around that obstacle. She began shipping boxes of toys and clothing to our babysitter's house or Mommy's school. No one was going to stop her from sending her grandbabies gifts. Mommy would sneak things into the house at different times so that he would not notice—he took inventory of anything that seemed new or different from clothes to toys. If he questioned anything, Mommy told him that she had purchased it but he did not remember. There was a time when he asked her directly if some recent "purchases" came from Mom Mom and Pop Pop. I knew Mommy was going to get it from him. In the calm tone she had rehearsed, she looked him square in the eye and smiled, saying, "I bought those clothes for the children yesterday. Remember? I was telling you, and you were half asleep."

"Oh, okay. You are right. I remember. I do not want nary a thing coming in here from that woman. She doesn't run my household. I do!"

Later that day, mommy informed us that she had to cool out for a while in bringing us anything new, but we would get all the packages eventually. He was a grown man but jealous because his parents never sent gifts to us for birthdays or otherwise.

He did not want us to have an ounce of love. I asked myself what his motivation was for the constant turmoil, the verbal, mental, and physical abuse toward us. Why would he deny his own children toys?

What I have come up with is fear.

Mrs. Spencer

"Now unto him that is able to keep you from falling and to present you faultless before the presence of His glory with exceeding joy. To the only wise God, our Savior, be glory and majesty, dominion, and power, both now and forever. Let all God's people say Amen."

With the benediction recited, Reverend Durham's service at Durham AME Zion Church in Bay Shore, New York, ended. Mommy began scooping up our sheets of scribbled doodling and candy wrappers.

"Who do these cute little babies belong to?"

Mommy was so busy picking up after us that she did not notice the apple-shaped, middle-aged woman trying to get her attention. The stately, navy-blue pillbox hat she wore matched her simply tailored, navy-blue suit. The ruffles of her collared blouse gently cascaded over her jacket collar. Her sweet, humble smile illuminated sparkly, brown eyes behind round glasses that focused on Robert and me. Her perfect diction could have been mistaken for an Englishwoman's. "Who is your mommy?" she asked while gently placing her pristine, white glove on Robert's head.

I gave Mommy's shirtdress a tug to get her attention. I liked to see her in the army-green dress, especially when she wore the thin, brown leather belt that made her small waist almost nonexistent. Her navy-blue, fitted blazer completed the schoolteacher look.

The woman asked, "Are these your babies?"

"Yes, ma'am, they are."

"What are their names?"

"Wendy and Robert," Mommy said proudly as she gently pulled us closer.

"How old are they? Are they in school yet?"

"Robert is four years old, and Wendy is three. No, ma'am, they are not in school yet."

"Well, why aren't they?" The question was asked as if Mommy had committed a misdemeanor.

"Well, ma'am, we just relocated to this area." Mommy's perfect posture became a slight hunch as she answered with an apologetic tone. Her dark-brown, almond-shaped eyes were cast downward.

"Well, welcome to Bay Shore. My name is Delores Spencer." She held out her gloved hand. Mommy shook it, and Robert and I did the same.

"My name is Mrs. Howell," Mommy said.

"Well, where are you from, and what prompted your move?"

"I'm from Laurel, Delaware. My husband and I relocated recently for work and live in Central Islip."

"What type of work do you do?" Mrs. Spencer's tone began to soften.

"We are both high school teachers, ma'am." I could tell that Mommy felt the genuine warmth of the woman's presence. Later, she told me that Mrs. Spencer's kindness reminded her of her own mother, who she missed tremendously.

"Well, where do the babies go during the day while you and your husband are teaching?" Slightly squinting while leaning her head to the side, Mrs. Spencer seemed confused and concerned.

"Right now, a neighbor is watching them until I can locate a suitable babysitter."

"Is the neighbor teaching them or just watching them, dear?"

Now it was mommy's turn to be puzzled by the question. "She watches them along with her own two children."

"Oh. Well, these children need to be in a learning environment. I take care of children from the community in my home. I have been doing it for many years. I not only care for them as if they were my own, but I teach them the alphabet, the number system, how to read and play well with others, and a host of other things. I have five children of my own who are in school. Previously, I taught in the local school system. I live here in Bay Shore, not too far from the church."

I could tell by the sparkle in Mommy's eyes and the smile that came across her face that she was impressed, if not overwhelmed. Although Mrs. Spencer seemed pushy asking one question after another, there was care and gentleness in her tone.

"I'm going to leave you with my name and number if you should change your mind." She scribbled the information on the church bulletin. "It was very nice to meet you, Mrs. Howell." Mrs. Spencer reached down to give our cheeks a soft tug and squeeze. "Take care of these precious babies." She exited the church, walking away with the grace of an English queen. Mommy already knew this was the right woman to care for her babies.

A first-class education was not an option—it was a necessity like food and water. Mrs. Spencer shared this belief for her own children, which was one of the many reasons she was selected to be our babysitter. The curriculum of the school district in our neighborhood was not up to our parents' high standards. Education was paramount in our household, and no matter where they had to go to get the best for us, they did. Mommy shared this concern with Mrs. Spencer, who graciously volunteered her address for registering us in school. Mrs. Spencer lived across the tracks in the town of Bay Shore where the schools were of a higher standard and the curriculum was more advanced than our schools. Throughout the majority of our school years, our friends thought we lived on Manatuck Boulevard. However, we lived in a town called Central Islip until we were in junior high school and then moved to Brentwood. On the weekends, if any friends dropped by, they were told that we were out with our mother. Every now and again when Mommy could arrange it, she dropped by Mrs. Spencer's house on the weekends for a visit, which allowed us to play with our friends from school who lived in the neighborhood.

While growing up, we often wished our house could be like Mrs. Spencer's. Her children's friends came over whenever they wanted, they had sleepovers, and they were able to go to the mall to hang out. They were allowed to receive and make phone calls to friends. With five children in the house, it seemed like there were always big birthday parties going on. Their summer vacations were spent traveling to North Carolina, Disney World, Fire Island, New York City, and many other places. They were also allowed to go to summer camp. Most importantly, they had a dog.

As the years passed, our fondness grew into love for Mrs. Spencer and the entire Spencer clan. Mrs. Spencer insisted that we call her Grandma and her husband Granddaddy. She made it clear she was not trying to take the place of our biological grandmother, whom we lovingly called Mom Mom. She treated us no different than her own five children. When we arrived in the mornings, she fed us breakfast. Even if we had already eaten, there was always room for a little more, as she would say. When we arrived home from school, we always had a snack of fruit, cookies, or a sandwich while we sat at her dining room table doing homework alongside her children.

Grandma was a disciplinarian. We could not play outside until everyone's homework was completed and checked. We had our own dresser drawer of old, faded, fringed jeans and T-shirts worn as play clothes that we changed into as soon as we arrived from school. Grandma made sure our school clothes were kept in pristine condition. A sandwich bag with multicolored barrettes was kept in our drawer in the back bedroom. I always seemed to manage to come home missing one or two, losing them at recess on the playground, but Grandma always kept a supply.

"Wendy, this is not the way your mother sent you to school this morning," she would say while examining my head, hands on her round hips. "Bring me the hair grease, comb, brush, and barrettes from the back room. We need to get this head together before your mother arrives." It seemed like Grandma rebraided my hair after school more often than I can remember.

William Spencer, whom we lovingly called Granddaddy, was a quiet man with a medium-brown complexion, a slightly oblong-shaped face, and piercing dark-brown eyes, and he always kept his hair cut close with tapered sides. With a six-foot-two, medium-build frame, he walked lightly but carried a big stick. He was a man of few words until he felt his children or family members were in harm's way, and then the man of few words roared like a lion. He worked as a chef at a local convent. However, in his earlier cooking career he was an executive chef on the president's dining car exclusively cooking for the president of the Penn Central Railroad as well as cooking for Mamie Doud Eisenhower who used the president's car when traveling. He could cook anything. On any given day, the aroma of bacon, collard greens, fried fish, rice, ham hocks, scrapple, okra, sweet potatoes, cabbage, succotash, sage sausage, grits, cheese eggs, pancakes, fried chicken, and other fare could be enjoyed.

Granddaddy was slow walking and slow talking. His big frame was intimidating to most, but we all knew he was a pussycat. Once I snatched a football from the boys after they would not let girls play. Miguel Gonzalez chased me and knocked me down to retrieve the ball. I ran in the house, crying to Granddaddy. He grabbed me by the hand and walked me to the side of the house where they were playing.

The rumbling roar of his voice was like an Amtrak train at full speed. "Heyyyy!"

He let my hand go, walked over to the huddle of twelve- and thirteen-year-old boys, snatched Miguel, and lifted him off the ground by his collar. The dangling of his mud-stained, black-and-white Pro Keds and the high pitch of his squealing voice sent everyone into uncontrollable laughter. Granddaddy tossed Miguel's scrawny body off to the side, where he lay like a deflated bag of trash on the side of the road.

"Don't you ever put your hands on my granddaughter again!" The deep roar of his voice froze everyone in place. "I don't want to see you back here again unless you know how to play right. Now get out of here!"

Miguel gained enough strength to run off the property at full speed, never looking back. As a sign of victory, I stuck my tongue out at him as he whizzed past. Granddaddy murmured a slur under his breath, turned around, and slowly retreated into the house.

CHAPTER 4

Mornings

Mornings were always hectic in our house when getting ready for school. This morning, Mommy made her usual wake-up call to our room: "Okay, children, it's time to wake up." Her voice was so soft and sweet. The tone gently massaged you out of your dreams with a smile.

"C'mon, babies, it is time to get up. Now who is going first?"

The warmth of the soft-knit, beige blanket over the crisp, white sheets kept me still. I had perfected the art of freezing in a fetal position, faking sleep. Robert would pull the covers tighter across his body. Most of the time, I could wait him out.

"Robert, do you wanna go first?" Mommy asked again in her sweet voice.

I remained motionless. A murmur came from across the room under the covers as Robert's body twitched.

"Your sister is still sleeping."

He flung his covers off and onto the floor. "No, she's not, Mom. Look at her over there." He shuffled slowly across the hardwood floor in his slippers to show his disgust, but the scraping of the brown, pressboard dresser drawers indicated he was searching for clean socks, underwear, and a T-shirt. As soon as he left for the bathroom, the lights went off, and my eyes flipped open. A smirk formed on my lips. Mommy usually allowed me a few more minutes before she returned. Mornings were not my forte, and I was always slow getting started.

The room was still dark, but I knew when she was near, as the sweet smell of her perfume was a dead giveaway. It made me want to smell pretty, just like her, whenever I entered a room. Slowly, as if not to awaken me, she opened the white dresser drawer to select my undergarments and tights. The creak of the bottom drawer meant she was selecting a blouse. By picking out parts of my outfit, she gave me a jumpstart on getting dressed.

"Wendy, Mommy's going to turn the lights on now." With her keen mother's intuition, she knew I was awake even when I thought she didn't know. Still, I would slowly roll over as if being newly awakened. I went through my entire theatrical routine. With outstretched arms, arching my back like a gazelle, I rose from under the covers, giving the Oscar-winning performance topped off with a wide yawn and an animalistic growl.

"Good morning, baby. How did Mommy's baby sleep?" The look in her eyes made me aware that she knew I had been awake for some time.

"Good," I replied as I sat on the side of the bed, stretching my feet to search for my favorite pink, furry bunny slippers. They kept my feet nice and toasty during the winter months. I asked the same question each morning. "Is he gone?"

"No but almost. He is outside warming up the cars. Hurry up and put your bathrobe on. Your brother should be coming out of the bathroom shortly."

Slowly, one arm at a time, I slipped on my pink, cotton bathrobe. Grabbing the ends of the sash, Mommy tied them into a knot around my waist. With the precision of a surgeon, she began separating my matted hair with her fingers. "Remind Mommy to put a few rollers in your hair tonight before you go to bed."

I had not gotten used to sleeping with curlers in my hair. Depending on how straight my hair was, Mommy would roll it tight. However, before lying down for the evening, I relieved the pressure on my scalp by unsnapping the pink plastic fasteners and loosening my hair from the pink foam.

The bedroom door swung open. We jumped.

It was only Robert. "Finished!" he shouted as he smiled in my direction, flashing his freshly brushed teeth, a hint of Scope mouthwash releasing into the air.

"Okay, baby." Mommy patted me on the back, moving me toward the door.

Most mornings consisted of a quick wash up since we took baths the night before. The routine was necessary, because he never gave us enough time in the morning to get ready. It was okay for him to spend hours in the bathroom but not Mommy or us—we were given twenty minutes. His ritual consisted of drinking a cup of coffee and reading the newspaper while on the toilet. That took at least thirty minutes. He then flushed and stood over the sink to shave. When we heard the sound of water gushing, he was headed for the shower. The paper-thin walls in the one-floor rental house left no sound unheard.

"Wendy," he'd shout out over the waterfall. "Is my uniform ready? I need some socks too! Pour me another cup of coffee so I can get out of here!"

The scent of Brut made us aware that he was out and his bathroom takeover came to an end.

"Hurry, get in the bathroom, and I'll be in to help." Mommy guided me out of our bedroom, closing the door behind her so Robert could get dressed.

In the mornings, Mommy dropped us off at Grandma Spencer's house so that we could catch the bus from the corner on Manatuck Boulevard. Despite our foot-dragging, Robert and I loved getting up in the morning and going to her house.

This morning, Mommy did not fix breakfast, which meant she would stop at the bagel shop along the way. We loved the bagel shop. The smell of onion bagels filled the car as we pulled up. At seven thirty, the lines had already begun to spill onto the street. It seemed like all of Brentwood had the same idea every morning.

"Okay, Robert, you and your sister go in and get three bagels with butter." Mommy parallel parked in front of the store.

"What kind do you want?" I asked, one leg already out the car door.

"It doesn't matter. Just get butter, no cream cheese. I don't have enough today."

"That's okay, Mom. I don't have to get one. I'm not hungry anyway." Robert was always ready to be the sacrificial lamb.

"We have enough, Robert." If anyone needed to make the sacrifice, Mommy made sure it was never one of her children. "Here." She handed Robert a crumpled five-dollar bill that looked as if it had gone a few turns in the washing machine. Robert was always given the money. Mommy said it was because he was older and he was the boy. I vowed that someday when I got older, I would be able to hold the money.

"How much change do you get back?"

A jolt of energy shot through me, as if I were competing for a prize on *The Price Is Right*. Her eyes darted between Robert and me, anticipating who would answer first. Robert looked down at the wrinkled bill, tilted his head back, and closed his eyes in silent calculation. Within seconds, he blurted, "Three fifty!" He was in fifth grade. I had not had a chance.

"Is he right?" Mommy's eyes shifted toward me in the back seat.

"Yup," I said, having no idea.

We bolted from the car. Patches of steam from the oven covered the bakery windows, rendering it hard to see inside. I was tempted to draw a picture on the steamed glass, but I knew I would endure a scolding by Mommy once I returned to the car if I did. The fresh-baked goodness of onion bagels swept me into a trance as I stood in line next to Robert. I was lost in images of me pulling apart the toasted bagel and slowly licking the dripping butter from the warm, soft, fluffy middle.

A poke to my elbow interrupted my thoughts. "Got a quarter?" Robert's dark-brown eyes were wide with anticipation.

"What do you need a quarter for? We have enough."

"I wanna surprise Mommy and get hers with cream cheese." His left hand opened to reveal one quarter and a piece of pocket lint.

"Wait a minute. Let me check."

Mommy would fuss about how we should save our money and not spend our change on her, but whenever we did, whether it was to buy her a card, perfume, candy, or some other small token of our love, she treasured it and told anyone who would listen what her babies did for her.

I always kept seventy-five cents or more in my pockets in case we went to the corner store after school for candy.

I unzipped the pocket of my tweed vest and pulled out all the change I had. Robert carefully selected two dimes and a nickel. The middle-aged, dumpy white woman behind the counter grew impatient. The scowl across her face made her thin lips disappear as she tapped her arthritic fingers on the glass counter. Robert handed her the change and grabbed our bag, and we raced back to the car. He handed the bagels out, careful not to pull out Mommy's.

"Did you get what you wanted?" she asked as she steered the Impala back onto the street.

"Yup. Thanks, Mom."

"You're welcome. Wendy, do me a favor and put the change in my purse in the side pocket."

Smiling at one another, we never let on that she had a surprise waiting for her in the bag when she arrived at school.

CHAPTER 5

Shaky

"S haky" was the name of Mommy's full-size, two-door, hard-toped, bullet-shaped, white 1965 Chevy Impala with the long tail span. The side windows were curved and frameless with chrome trim on the outside and inside. The pleated, vanilla-colored vinyl seats stuck to our thighs in the summer and made them shiver with a shock of chill in the winter. Shaky was the hand-me-down car that he gave her. Mommy always got the used cars, never the new ones, even though her money and credit had to be used for the purchase, because she had the stronger credit score. This season, the Long Island winters seemed more severe and raw compared to years past.

"How come you always get the old car whenever we get new cars?" Robert asked Mommy one morning as she was loading us into the car.

"Well, baby, old cars are better. Shaky is broken in and reliable. You never know what you're going to get with those new cars."

Mommy always had a graceful way of deflecting from the truth that she had been bamboozled by him. It made my insides boil, because I knew that once again, she was covering for his unwavering self-worship and lack of giving a damn about anyone but himself.

This was another cold morning ride to Grandma Spencer's house. Every morning, Mommy carefully wrapped the multicolored crocheted patchwork blankets around Robert and me, preparing us for the twenty-five-minute journey. She lay a heavier blanket across us for extra warmth. She handed us the vintage, red-and-black plaid Aladdin thermos with a red cup that Grandma Spencer had given us and that Mommy faithfully filled with piping-hot Swiss Miss hot chocolate every morning.

The smile on her face each morning, as she carefully wrapped us, was a mask of pain and shame. It was the pain she felt every time she had to place us in that frozen steel bullet.

Sometimes Shaky stalled out, and it took a few tries to restart her. If Mommy got too anxious and tried too many times, Shaky flooded out. Those were the times when we had to play the waiting game before she attempted to start Shaky again. Those were the times that the hot chocolate came in handy. Shaky's radio worked well, and the way the tunes busted out made you think you were at your own private concert. Robert and I took turns asking Mommy to turn to our favorite station. Mommy played the singing game with us, asking us to sing along to every song. We loved it, not suspecting this was her way to pass the time and take our minds off the fact that we were sitting in a cold, steel bullet that wouldn't start. We loved the singalongs, never realizing we did not have any heat.

During the summer months, Mommy kept a gallon of water stored in a plastic container in the trunk. One day, smoke started to rise from under the hood. One of our neighbors, Mr. Johnson, came over and said the car was overheating. He showed Mommy how to pour water in the radiator to cool it off. Apparently, there was a pinhole-sized leak in a hose, which led to water slowly leaking out. If the reservoir was not checked each time she started Shaky, the car could overheat. From that point on throughout the summer, she made sure to carry a gallon of water in the trunk in case we got stuck.

Mommy could not take any money from the kitty to have Shaky fixed, because he opened the bottom dresser drawer in their bedroom, removed the worn envelope, and counted it faithfully every day. The lion's share of the emergency fund money saved was hers, but he allowed her only a stipend of one hundred dollars every two weeks when she got paid, which was not enough money to buy groceries and incidentals for Robert and me. Mommy always found a way to make the pennies stretch.

"Why is this damn car overheating?" he yelled one school morning as he came into the house after starting the cars.

"She never overheated on me," Mommy lied. We all silently said a prayer that he did not open the trunk and find the stashed gallon of water.

"You are so muthafuckin' stupid, you wouldn't know if she was overheating or not! Your dumb ass wants a new car? Shit, you can't even take care of the one yah got!" He was screaming so loud that I knew the Johnsons were listening from their patio, and so did he. He prided himself whenever the opportunity was presented—and it was often—to demean us in public. He was the king of his castle, as he dutifully reminded us, and this king ruled over all beneath him.

Later in life, after working in several social service jobs, I learned that his behavior was typical for abusers, a perverse sign of power and control. Demeaning a person is a way of stripping them naked of any self-worth that they had, making them feel inferior and worthless to the abuser, who is seen as the power keeper.

"Robert Howell, get me some water, and bring it out to me," he yelled at Junior as he slammed the front screen door behind him and stomped down the front steps. Junior was a nickname for Robert since he shared the same first and middle name of our father. I shared the first name of our mother.

Junior quickly ran and filled an eight-ounce Styrofoam cup with water. Mommy was standing at the screen door and held it open for him. Careful not to spill a drop, Junior handed him the cup. *Splash!* He snatched the cup out of Robert's hand and sent it crashing to the pavement. "You better bring me some goddamn water like I asked you to!"

Robert was fast as lightning, just escaping the raised foot meant to kick him as he reached down for the cup.

"Hurry up. I gotta get the hell out of here and git to work!"

By the time Robert ran back inside, Mommy and I were in the kitchen, frantically searching for a container that would hold more water. We guessed that was what he wanted. Of course, he never gave explicit directions. We had to read his mind to figure out what he wanted, and God help us if we interpreted an order incorrectly. He would say, "Figure it out. I shouldn't have to tell your dumb asses every damn thing." It was yet another way he controlled our minds.

"Will this be good?" I said as I retrieved an empty Ragu jar, tossed in the trash the night before.

"No, baby, not glass!" The look of sheer fear plastered on her face told me that she did not want to take any chance of a glass jar being thrown at Robert.

"Hurry up, Mom, before he comes in." Robert's voice trembled with fear.

Mommy open and slammed the cabinets under the kitchen sink in disgust. She could not find what she wanted. She swung open the refrigerator door, snatched out the milk carton, held it up to her right ear, and shook it. She opened the spout and, with one eye closed, peered inside as if looking for treasure. "Hurry up, drink this!" she said as she handed the carton to Robert.

Robert grabbed it out of her hand, gulped down the milk, and handed the empty carton back to her.

"Where is that boy?" His roaring voice echoed from the front door to the back of the house where we cowered in the kitchen. His face was pressed against the screen door like a Peeping Tom, and the whites of his eyes were growing red.

The milk carton held under the faucet was overflowing into Mommy's hands. She quickly grabbed a dish towel to wipe off the water from around the carton and then handed it to Robert. "Careful, don't spill it." She wiped a drop of milk from the corner of his mouth.

Robert hustled toward the screen door. "Here I come, sir." His voice was a shaky whimper.

"There better be enough water in there. Is there?" He snatched the carton out of Robert's hand.

"Yes, sir."

I hated saying "Yes, sir" and "No, sir" to him. It made me feel subservient. In reality, of course, we all were. It was embarrassing to have to say it in public. People looked at us with weird expressions of uncertainty and pity. He said we had to call him sir because that was what his father demanded of him. Didn't he know how low we felt whenever I answered him, like how slaves felt in the company of their ever-present masters? Of course, he knew. It was all part of his plan.

After he poured the water in the radiator, he got behind the wheel. Thankfully, Shaky started right up. We all breathed a sigh of relief as we loaded in the car, Mommy drove us to Grandma's house, and he drove away in the new car.

CHAPTER 6

Report Card

Besides the last day of school, report card time was one of the worst times of the school year for my brother and me.

"If you come home with anything less than a C, do not come home." That threatening phrase was always in the front of our minds. The words implanted fear in Robert and me to strive for excellence. Robert did well in his studies, easily earning A's and B's. Algebra, trigonometry, calculus—you name it, it came naturally to him.

I excelled in English, foreign language, and social studies but struggled with math. Anything after algebra, and it was a wrap. Robert tried to tutor me and offer shortcuts to memorize formulas. Sometimes it worked, but usually it did not.

He told Robert and me that one of his greatest fears in life was his children growing up and being "nothings in life."

Robert later became a career serviceman. He traveled the world, putting his life on the line fighting, teaching other servicemen and women, and serving his country domestically and abroad during his twenty-plus years in the United States Marines. Now he works full time while remaining active serving in the United States Army Reserve and is married with children.

I earned a bachelor's and master's degrees, owned and operated a small errand service business while in grad school, managed investment property, and served as a missionary in the Dominican Republic. I worked alongside medical professionals who travelled to remote communities, setting up mobile clinics to treat poverty-stricken families. I work full time, and as of this publication, I am a successful, published author with *The New York Times* bestseller list in my sight.

So much for being "nothings."

When we were young, he said we were going to get our education no matter what, even if he had to beat it into us.

He reminded us how hard he had it when growing up. He worked on a farm until nightfall every day after school and was still expected to maintain straight As. He said we had it easy, because we did not know what hard work was and did not appreciate what we had. I imagine my father felt trapped on that farm. Perhaps because of this, he felt cheated out of life and therefore instilled in us a desire for more, which he felt we would achieve only through education. He was a college graduate and became a schoolteacher, athletic director, and high school football and track coach. He left the farm life behind, returning only occasionally to visit family.

We never saw his report cards and the straight As he bragged about. However, we did see the college degree that hung in his parents' house in Maryland. Mommy used to tell me how he spent long hours studying in the college library, went to football or track practice, and then returned home to work on the farm.

"You chillen have it toooooo damn easy," he said. "You don't know what it's like to run a tractor and work in the fields in the scorching hot summer sun and cold winters." Well, that was not true, because we got plenty of doses of it.

During the summer break from school, he often dragged us down to Salisbury to work in the unforgiving summer sun without protection for our heads or bodies against the scorching rays. I remember going down to that dusty farm from second to twelfth grade. It was torture.

Yes, his life had been torture. My father's father was an abuser, and it was passed down to my father.

Robert and I swore we would break the cycle. Not every victim of child abuse abuses their own children. Robert never has and never will.

"Sooo, how are you chillen doing in school?" he asked from time to time in his fake Southern accent.

I hated it when he spoke that way. I think he did it because he said he was a country boy. Yes, he was raised in Maryland. The exaggerated, manufactured, country, ignorant-sounding accent was quickly lost upon relocation to Long Island where living in a predominately white neighborhood brought the Southern fakeness to a screeching halt. He was too busy trying to impress the white people. He switched off in the country lingo only when inside the house or around some of his Masonic Brothers.

"How are dem grades comin'?"

Depending on who had enough nerve, one of us would answer. This time it was me. "Okay," I said in a fearful tone.

"What kind of grades am I to be 'spectin? I hope As and Bs. You know if you bring home any Cs what will happen to ya, dontcha?" A slow, vengeful smile spread across his face. "Ya might as well not even come the fuck home." He looked to Robert. "Hey little fella, what about you? Cat got your tongue or somethin'?"

"No, sir," Robert said with trepidation.

Of course, we were lying. What were we supposed to do? Tell the truth and get beaten before the main event? Might as well take one beating when the report card came. There was no sense in enduring two. I don't know what was worse: elementary or high school report cards.

Parent-teacher nights were held shortly before receiving the report cards. Waiting at Grandma and Granddaddy's house for him and Mommy to pick us up kept Robert and me on pins and needles. Grandma Spencer tried to keep us occupied with dinner and watching television, but it did not make the waiting any easier. Finally, the bright white headlights of his car shone through the living room curtains. My heart dropped, and my stomach ached. I tried to measure his anger level by the slam of the door. A few endless seconds passed, and the doorbell rang.

Grandma Spencer slowly rose from the sofa to answer. "Children, get yourselves ready. That's your mother." She spoke softly.

"Hi ya, Mrs. Howell. How are you feelin'?" Grandma asked in a warm, cheerful tone.

"I'm doing fine, Mrs. Spencer. How are you this evening? I hope we're not too late."

"Oh, get on in here. Everything is fine. The children have had their dinner and done their homework, which I checked. I just gave them a little snack."

"Thank you so much, Mrs. Spencer, I really appreciate it," said Mommy.

"Did you eat? I have plenty of fried chicken, mashed potatoes, and fresh string beans from the garden." Grandma and Grandaddy Spencer had a fabulous garden. Every day when Grandaddy came home from work, he headed straight to his garden. He meticulously watered and tilled each row with great care and was proud of his crops.

Sometimes Grandma Spencer watched him from the kitchen window and proudly said, "That man loves his garden." Many times, he brought in the vegetables to cook for dinner and placed them in the sink for Grandma to wash and prepare. It was nothing to see light-green tomatoes carefully placed in a row to line the white kitchen windowsill. The morning sun that shined through the window naturally ripened them to a bright red.

Sometimes Grandaddy let us pick up the green garden hose and spray the water as he directed us like a choir conductor. "Careful! Let up on the handle. Do not spray so hard! Spray up!"

Working in his garden brought a relaxing peace after work each day.

"Why don't you sit and have some?" Grandma Spencer asked.

"Oh no, Mrs. Spencer. I would not want to put you through so much trouble. He is waiting for us in the car."

Grandma Spencer knew Mommy would say no, but she always offered, hoping one day she would get a yes. Mommy always said no when he was around. The one time when she said yes, he beat her so badly that she went to school the next day with a slight limp.

"Children, hurry up and get your coats on. Your mother is waiting," Grandma Spencer called. "How were the fifth and sixth grade teacher conferences, Mrs. Howell?"

"Okay for the most part. Wendy just needs to stop talking so much in class," Mommy said in a cautious tone.

"Well, children will do that at times," Grandma Spencer said.

I could tell by the worrisome look on Mommy's face that it went deeper. We said our goodbyes, walking slowly to the car where he waited. The cold, hollow, piercing glare that he gave me through the windshield let me know that my time had come to face his wrath. The driver's side door opened, and he got out. He stared at me as he folded the black leather seat forward for me and Robert to climb in the back.

"Hi, baby doll. How is Daddy's girl?" The forced, half-crooked smile was a telling sign of what was to come. The fakeness of his tender voice was only for show because Grandma Spencer was standing in her doorway, witnessing our departure. Oh, how I wished I lived with the Spencers.

Slowly, he backed his army-green, 1978 Monte Carlo out of the driveway. He gave the horn two quick beeps as the car picked up speed down Manatuck Boulevard toward Pine Aire drive. He made a sharp right turn and continued racing down Fifth Avenue. As we sped past Durham AME Zion Church, I said a quick, silent prayer for mercy.

"So, Wendy, whooooo issssss Bettina Traylor?" he asked slowly in a soft, sinister voice. Bettina Traylor was one of the cool girls in my fifth grade class.

"A girl in my, my, my—" I stuttered. The pain of his quick punch to my mouth brought stars to my eyes. My head smacked against the back seat.

"Robert, the tree!" Mommy screamed, helpless.

"Shut the fuck up. Was I talking to you, bitch? I know how the fuck to drive! Now hold this fucking wheel straight!" he yelled as he turned around and delivered two quick, closed-fist blows, one square to my face and one to my mouth. He turned around and snatched the wheel from Mommy's grasp. As soon as Mommy turned around to look at me, she was met with a quick blow to the head. "Turn the fuck around! Turn the fuck around I said!" He grabbed a handful of her hair, snatching her head around.

Mommy held up both hands, trying to protect her face. "Robert, please! Please!"

I was not sure if the blood was coming from my nose, my mouth, or both, but the warm taste in my mouth curdled in my stomach, making me feel sick.

"I dare you to go back to school now and talk in class!" he threatened.

I felt two taps on my left hand. It was Robert. I snuck a quick look at him in of my peripheral vision so as not to be seen by the glaring black eyes piercing through me in the rearview mirror. Robert motioned with his right hand for me to put my head back. The blood in my mouth was coming from my nose. I slowly placed my head back and up, but the flow of the blood down my throat was making me silently gag. Robert's grasp on my hand tightened.

As the Monte Carlo pulled up into the L-shaped driveway, I began to feel my panties getting wet. As much as I crossed my legs and clenched my thighs and buttocks, the water kept coming. Thankfully, he exited the car quickly. In that moment, I wished Mommy could have jumped in the driver's seat, backed up, and sped far away, but his frame loomed in the doorway.

"Wendy, take her in the bathroom and clean her up! Then get your ass ready for bed!" He shouted in my direction. He walked into the house and slammed the door behind him, leaving us in the car.

"Sis, I'll get your bag." Robert spoke softly. He always looked after me. He sniffed and looked at me for confirmation.

"I peed on myself," I said fearfully.

"Just get up slow," he said in the most comforting tone.

"Robert, here. You take these and wipe the seat when she gets up," Mommy said as she handed Robert a wad of tissues from her purse.

"Sis, you have to get out so I can wipe the seat."

As soon as I pushed the driver's seat forward and placed one foot out of the car, the stream of pee ran down my legs and over my white cotton knee socks. Robert handed me my book bag and wiped the seat.

"Baby, go to the bathroom, and I will be right in." Mommy's voice trembled.

Tears welled up in my eyes, but they would not fall.

As soon as we all entered, he shouted, "What is that smell? Wendy, do I smell piss? Did that girl pee on herself again? Looka here, she better not have peed in my damn car, or I know something. I don't know why that goddamn girl can't hold her piss."

In the bathroom, Mommy asked me to lean forward against her as I stepped out of my favorite navy-blue pleated skirt. She slowly unbuttoned the back of my ruffle-collared blouse and removed it from my body. "Baby, lift your arms for Mommy," she whispered as she pulled my bloodied T-shirt over my head.

Laying my left hand on her shoulder, I bent down to remove my urine-soaked knee socks. The flow of blood from my nose made a puddle at my feet.

"Baby, hold your head back for Mommy," she said as she gently tilted my chin up.

After searching the drawer under the sink, she found some cotton balls, slowly rolled one in her hand, and placed it up my nose. She reached for another and repeated the steps. Once satisfied with her work, she went over to the tub and turned on the water. She picked up the pink Mr. Bubble box and sprinkled white powder into the warm water. Suds bubbled to the surface.

"Wendy!" His shriek made Mommy and me jump with fear. "What are we having for dinner? Pour me a drink," he demanded from down the hall.

"Baby, let the tub fill up halfway, and then get in. Mommy will be back."

She was gone long enough for me to bathe completely and dry myself off. I placed the urine-soaked clothes in the wicker clothes hamper under the window. I did not have any clean clothes in the bathroom, and my bathrobe was in my room. Slowly, I opened the bathroom door to peek out, and I saw Robert's light underneath his bedroom door across the hall. He was still up like I knew he would be.

I listened intently for my father's snoring down the hall in the family room. As usual, he ate, drank his vodka, and went to sleep. Softly, I cleared my throat, my eyes fixed on Robert's door.

No response. I did it again, a bit louder. Robert's door cracked open, allowing just enough light to escape to illuminate my path in the dark hallway. His shadowy form hovered behind the door. He stuck his hand out to motion for me to come. Carefully, I switched the light off in the bathroom, opened the bathroom door wider, and tiptoed across the hallway, following the pathway of light to my room. I was careful not to allow the floor to squeak under foot and wake the monster on the couch.

Once inside in the darkness, I changed into my pink cotton nightgown. After getting dressed, I tiptoed over to the wall that joined my room and Robert's. I tapped two times, letting my brother know that I was dressed and going to bed. Two soft taps returned.

I crawled into bed, wondering if the swelling of my nose and lips would go down by morning.

CHAPTER 7

The Aftermath

ooking from the outside, some would say we were weak, incapacitated to action. In many ways, we were helpless to his dictatorship. My mother, Junior, and I believed we were powerless against his tyranny, with no option to be free unless we placed others in jeopardy, and that was not an option. Whenever he promised us a thrashing, he made good on his word. We were not going to bring the same to our family and others we loved.

What outsiders could not see was that psychologically, we were growing strong. Having the ability to regulate our emotions, manage our thought processes, and behave positively despite our circumstances took a supreme mental toughness. To endure the frequent thrashings and other kinds of twisted abuse and not come out on the other side an addict or caught up in a lifestyle of doom and gloom was a triumph of will. Survival of the fittest. We operated by an unproven faith that we would be okay no matter what happened, even if we did not know how we would arrive at that okay place.

I awoke to hear the shower running. Mommy must have already been up. I placed my hand to my nose and pulled the cotton ball out. The dried blood was a sign that the bleeding had stopped during the night.

I got out of bed and made my way to the full-length mirror for a closer look at my lip. It was still a little swollen.

Gingerly, I gently pulled my bottom lip out to check the damage. It was stiff and sore, and the inside revealed two pus-filled, aching bumps. I practiced slowly turning my bottom lip inward to disguise the swelling. I would keep my lip tucked in throughout the day in school. I had become a pro at disguising welts, swollen limbs, bruises, and any other visible damage. Long sleeves and tights covered swellings and bruises. At other times, Mommy dotted and rubbed Fashion Fair foundation on my face to cover the black-and-blue bruises.

A light tap came to my wall—Junior was up and wanted to know if I was. I lightly tapped back. I sat back down on the edge of the bed and wondered if my father was going to finish me off with another beating before he left for work. The sound of the shower ended. I quickly slid back under the covers and pretended to be asleep. The light of the hallway entered my bedroom inch by inch as the door opened. I thought, *He is coming in to finish me off.* I braced myself and curled up in a fetal position to withstand the blows.

"Hey, baby." The sweet sound of Mommy's voice was music to my ears.

I softly cried out, "Mommy?"

"Yes, baby, he's gone." She sat next to me and gently pulled the covers down from my body. She tried to uncoil my tightly wound body, softly rubbing her hands down my sides. "It's okay. He's gone."

I slowly unfolded and relaxed.

"Mommy is going to turn the light on so I can get a look at your face." When she turned the light on, I saw Junior in the background.

"Hey, sis." The pitiful, helpless look on his face revealed the endless hurt I knew he was feeling for me.

"Robert, go in the kitchen for Mommy and put a few cubes of ice in a Ziploc bag and—"

He darted out of my bedroom before she could complete her request. He knew just what she wanted, having done this many times before. "I want you to lie here and keep the ice on your mouth. I will come and get you after your brother is out of the bathroom. You can wash up, and I will lay your clothes out."

Junior arrived with the bag of ice cubes. I winced at the cold against my sore mouth.

"Try to keep it pressed on there." The warmth of her touch on top of my hand was comforting. "Let me finish getting ready. I will come and get you when the bathroom is free."

CHAPTER 8

The Robber

My parents purchased a house in a better neighborhood. Robert and I had our own bedrooms. We resembled the Cosbys on the outside: two professional, degreed parents, living on a Long Island suburb in a fifteen-room house. On the inside, our lives were filled with threats and daily beatings. With alcohol introduced into the mix, the physical, mental, and verbal violence intensified, and the emotional instability was horrifying. An order was barked, twenty minutes later it changed, and we were blamed for his changed thoughts. Our childhoods were filled with terror and lies, and I vowed that I would never be like the monster abuser.

My father loved watching George Jefferson from the sitcom *The Jeffersons*. He marched and growled around our house with the same short, stout stature, spewing orders like George Jefferson. He consistently treated my mother, brother, and me like hired help.

The abuse continued, as best I can remember, from the ages of five to eighteen when I left for college. My brother, mother, and I were kicked, punched, slapped, stomped, shoved, and thrown. These beatings were coupled with verbal abuse, manipulation, intimidation, humiliation, and degradation. The constant anxiety kept us on our toes, trying to anticipate his next move.

My mom snuck in normal childhood experiences whenever she could determine his ever-changing schedule. We played Monopoly or Trouble with each other. She let us call friends from school or arranged timed visits to meet them at the South Shore Mall. She took us to the Carvel ice cream shop in town to indulge in a soft-serve black-and-white cone with sprinkles.

One Saturday, during one of those Carvel runs, Robert said he had come to a decision. "Mom, you and Wendy are girls, and your bodies cannot handle him like mine can." His chivalrous tone was far beyond sixth grade. "I will take most of his hits and punches."

"Robert, I am the mother. You do not have to take most of anything, because I will."

Mom's stern tone was out of character for her. Mom decided that his chivalry would not do, because as a mother, it was her responsibility to protect her young. It would be her who endured the punches, stomps, and slaps. "When the time is right, I will alert Mom Mom, and you two will go to Delaware and not look back." She knew we would be safe from hurt and danger there and well looked after. She would call ahead to her mother and make the arrangements. Little did she know that the outcome would be different.

"But Mom, remember when he said he would kill Mom Mom and Pop Pop?" I reminded her of his constant threats toward her family if we divulged how he was treating us and they tried to intercede. That plan of escape would not bode well for our grandparents, whom we loved dearly. Coupled with the daily beatings, that man drilled into us how he would kill our grandparents, aunts, and uncles if we spoke about the mistreatment. His threats were real. He kept a fully loaded Marlin 35 hunting rifle in the hall closet and was not afraid to use it.

"We all leave together, Mom, or not at all." That was the first time I heard Robert expressing a defiant tone toward her.

"Yes, Mom, all of us have to be together," I said.

"Okay, children, we will see." Whenever Mom responded "we will see," it was pretty much a done deal. She just needed to work things out.

Years ago, in the bathroom in the middle of the night, Robert heard a sound and quietly moved to the bathroom window. He crouched behind the white clothes hamper, pulled back the curtain, and peered out the window. There was a moving shadow behind Mommy's burnt orange-and-white 1977 Chevrolet Monte Carlo coupe with the weird rear "aero" window. He snuck across the bathroom floor, bent over, careful not to stand up and allow his shadow to be seen from the outside.

He cracked open my bedroom door. "Hey, sis," he whispered, "you wake?"

"Yeah," I whispered, "I'm awake." I sat upright, throwing the pink comforter off to the side, and readied to climb out of the bed.

"Somebody's outside behind Mom's car." He closed the door, crept to my bedside, and crouched down to my level. "It's a robber."

"What are you gonna do?" My voice was trembling.

"I'm gonna go and tell Dad."

"No, don't do that," I pleaded.

"I'm scared something is gonna happen to Mommy's car." His voice trembled too.

I swung my feet from under the comforter onto the white shag rug. The moonlight shone through my window, showing Robert's deliberate stare.

"Get back in bed, sis. It's gonna be okay. Just be quiet and pretend to be sleep. Hurry up so I can go." He gave my legs two quick taps, meaning I should get back under the covers.

Unhappily, I obliged. I was not sure what Robert's motives were to risk telling our father about the robber. Maybe he wanted to protect Mommy's car, knowing that it was the only transportation she had for us. Maybe it was more. I lay in bed, silently praying for my mother and brother's safety.

Whispered voices came closer outside my bedroom door. "Hurry up and get your shoes on." My father's authoritative whisper to Robert scared me so much I wanted to pee. Why he would involve Robert was beside me.

"Yes, sir." Robert had no choice but to go when he was summoned. Resistance would have been futile.

My mind raced. Robert saw one robber, but who was to say there weren't more?

Mommy quietly pushed my bedroom door open and got in bed with me, holding me tight to her bosom. The authoritative whispering continued down the hallway and then faded. I could sense someone under my bedroom window. I squeezed my arms around Mommy even tighter. Was it the robber under my window? Was there more than one? Was it Robert and my father? The fear rose inside my gut.

Pow, pow, pow, pow!

The Marlin 35 rifle was deafening. I clenched my legs so tight to stop the pee from streaming down them that they went numb. Where was Robert? That was my only thought. I could tell by her look of fear that Mommy was thinking the same.

"He will be all right," she whispered, "God is covering him."

Slam!

The kitchen door shut, then silence. Minutes seemed like hours as I lay in my mother's arms, waiting for a sign of Robert's safe return.

"Go get yourself cleaned up, and get in bed," my father barked. "Wendy, where you at?"

"Baby, I'll be back," she whispered as she gently removed her arm from around me and quickly left my room.

Two light taps came from Robert's wall. I threw the comforter off, jumped out of bed, and returned two quick taps to the wall, relieved that he was safe. Minutes later, I heard a faint police siren and then a knock at the front door. I jumped out of bed and cracked my bedroom door just enough to hear.

"Good evening, sir."

"Good evening, officers. How can I help you?"

"We received a call of a disturbance."

"Yes, officer. I was on my way to the bathroom when I noticed a glare of a light at my window. When I looked out, there were two shadows kneeling by the side of my wife's car. I grabbed my gun and went around the back of the house and fired a shot to scare them off."

"Well, that explains the gas cap on the floor by the side of the car. You must have hit one of them, because there was a small splatter of blood by the car."

"Well, officer, I wasn't aiming to hurt no one."

"They came on your property, and you were protecting your home. Looks like they were trying to siphon gas. Is everyone in the home okay?"

"Oh yes, officer. My family is fine."

"Did you get a chance to see their faces?

"No, officer."

"Okay. We'll check around the house, but looks like they're long gone by now. Also looks like you'll have to replace that cap."

"Yes, officer. Will do so in the morning."

"Probably a flesh wound. There were just a few dots of blood in the driveway. They deserved what they got for trespassing on private property. Heh, heh. Probably some illegals, ya know?"

"Yeah. Heh, heh. That is what I was thinking, officer. Got to protect my family."

"Yes, sir. Well, you lock up and have a good night. You and your wife have a good evening."

"Thank you, officers. You as well."

I quickly slid across the floor and jumped back in bed.

CHAPTER 9

Check Out

As schoolteachers, they were paid every two weeks. He had Mommy turn over her money after she cashed her check and gave her $100 for groceries, to pay Grandma Spencer for caring for us, to keep gas in her car, and other expenses for Robert and me. It was never enough.

At least once a week, he sent Mommy to Kentucky Fried Chicken or Burger King if he knew we were having leftovers. Mommy would ask him for money, and he would berate her, calling her stupid because she did not know how to budget all the money he gave her.

Still, Mommy always made it work. Sometimes she suggested fast food if she knew one of her students was working at a local fast-food chain. When she handed the cashier the money, they always gave her much more than what she had ordered. All her students loved her. She was the teacher who cared, sometimes the mother figure and confidante they did not have. She had to do what she had to do to get by and to protect us.

Mommy was an educated woman with a BA in Business Administration from University of Maryland Eastern Shore, yet she placed herself last on the list of priorities when it came to him. Through the Future Business Leaders of America Club (FBLA), she taught high school students at Central Islip High School how to run their own businesses, and she supervised the school store where the students sold candy and school supplies between class periods and during study hall. She coached the cheerleading squad. She had a keen, innate understanding that students learned at different paces and in different ways. This understanding led her to stay after school for a student who needed extra help.

Coaches would come to her, asking her to pass the star of their team so he could stay on the team. Mommy would stay after school with any student for as long as it took or come in early, but she never gave anyone a free pass. She was firm, and the students respected her for spending the extra time. Their mothers baked cakes, cookies, and casseroles. They brought potted plants or anything that they thought would encourage her to stay at school after the other teachers went home. Mommy graciously rejected the offerings, only to find them on her desk when she came to class the next day. Little did they know that none of these were necessary. She did it for the love of her students and the love of teaching.

Sometimes on Saturdays, when the school was open for sporting events, she packed my brother and me into the car. We would sit in the back of her classroom, Room 209, and do our homework, doodle, or read *Highlights* magazine while she worked with a student who was in jeopardy of being kicked off of the football, basketball, or track team and needed to pass her class to graduate. She called it "extra credit."

Whenever we accompanied her to school for parent-teacher night, we sat in the back of the class where we could overhear parents thanking her for going the extra mile for their children. Maybe she'd offered to stay late so that the challenged learners could complete their assignments or allowed the student to sit in on the same class during a different period of the day if they were not catching on.

Some came bearing a token of appreciation like a potted plant. She did not dare bring them home, because he forbade us from accepting anything from someone who showed a genuine interest in us. He said there was always an alternative motive and the person couldn't care less about us. She left the plants in her classroom for her and the students to enjoy, and she shared the baked goods with Robert, me, and the parents who came in to see her.

Sometimes her students accompanied their parents. Sometimes they came to talk to us and share what a great teacher they had in Mrs. Howell. Not only did she teach them, she also looked after their welfare. If they missed too many classes, she called their home to check on their whereabouts or stopped by for a visit. She provided a non-judgmental ear for their stories of family stress, school struggles, dating, and other issues.

For all this help, they sometimes paid her back. She did not want it, but sometimes she felt she had no choice. One girl named Rosa worked at Pathmark supermarket. When Mommy knew she was working on a Saturday, we would be sure to go. Once inside the market, our first order of business was to casually walk past each register as Mommy looked for Rosa. As soon as she made eye contact, she gave an enthusiastic wave.

Rosa found us in the dairy aisle. "Hi, Mrs. Howell. I am going on my lunch break, so take your time. I have an hour. You brought your coupons, right?"

I proudly held up the coupon box.

"Wow, you got a lot! Good, 'cause today is double coupon day. Put all the high ones on top."

After an hour and a half, we pushed the grocery cart into Rosa's Lane. When she was done ringing us up, the bill was a little over $100. I was worried.

"Ma'am, do you have any coupons?" Rosa asked as she addressed mommy as a customer.

Mommy handed over the coupons, and Rosa rang them up: a coupon for one dollar off Alpo dog food for our imaginary dog. We had one dollar off Clairol hair dye, and three one-dollar coupons for Tide laundry detergent. Rosa swiped coupons for things that I had never heard of in addition to the ones I had cut out that morning. With every swipe of a coupon, I bagged faster, packing the meats next to the paper towels instead of in their own bag the way Mommy taught me. It did not matter as long as we got the groceries in there and got out of Pathmark quickly.

By the time Rosa completed swiping the coupons, our bill decreased from a little over $100 to a little over $50. Mommy paid.

"Have a nice day, ma'am, and thank you for bagging."

As we started down Wicks Avenue, Mommy broke her silence. "Your father gives me fifty dollars a week from the kitty for groceries. That barely covers the meats he wants. That does not include the cold cuts to make sandwiches for lunches during the week, canned goods, sodas, liquor, vegetables, detergent, and fish when he asks for it. You know I make it stretch most of the time, cutting back and hoping he does not notice. We need to make sure I come home with everything he asks for or else—"

She did not need to finish the sentence. We knew how that sentence ended: *or else he will beat us all.*

CHAPTER 10

Master Lodge

"Boy, you sure got them children trained right."

Mr. James Wilson was one of his Masonic Lodge brothers, and he always said this when he came over for free liquor and a meal. Oftentimes his slick-ass comments left a negative taste that instigated a fight between my father and mother when he left. He was a tall, dark-skinned man, and his voice sounded as if he was half tipsy. He was never without his brown-tinted glasses to cover his bloodshot eyes. He hailed from a town in Suffolk County called Wyandanch, and most of his kids were "wayward," as he said. One of his two sons was flunking out of school and smoked weed in their basement with his girlfriend when his parents were not home. The other son was a star high school running back. He was being groomed to be an NFL player but succumbed to the drug scene as a dealer, which cancelled his father's big retirement dreams. That left his daughter, fifteen-year-old Angie, a punk rocker, which was taboo for a black kid. She wore a spiked nose ring with multiple matching spiked earrings in both ears, thick black lipstick, black nail polish, Levi's jeans with holes in both knees, a fringed white T-shirt, black leather vest, green combat boots, and a jet-black mohawk. Prior to graduating high school, she was saddled with a baby and a dead end, no hope. That left his youngest, Myesha, who was the smartest of them all. After college, she married and moved out of town, returning only for holidays.

"My wife doesn't do like yours. Brother, how you do it?" Mr. Wilson would ask.

"Hey, if she don't say what I want to hear, I just tear that ass up." The cocky tone in my father's voice tone curdled my stomach. Mommy wore her masked, plastered smile at the sound of yet another demeaning insult to her face. "Right, Wendy?" he said, looking at her for acknowledgment of his degrading comment.

"Yes, Robert, you are right."

I know it killed her to reply that way.

I hated when company was around. He bragged about his finances, education, military, and job status while sloshing back the vodka Mommy served to him and his Masonic brothers. I am sure there were probably some Masons who did some good in the community, but not in this bunch. These were adulterers, drunkards, and skirt-chasing philanders. They held all-day-and-night, closed-door meetings in New York City if not every Sunday then every other Sunday. Throughout the year, they sold tickets for functions like dances, cabarets, casino trips, boat trips, formal balls, and anything else that involved liquor, women, music, and fun, in that order. They announced themselves at one another's homes with a secret knock and once inside, greeted each other with a secret handshake. Every once in a while, when there were non-Masons in their presence, they spoke to each other in code.

From what I could see, it was all a bunch of shit. This lodge was nothing but a front to leave the wives at home so that they could philander around in New York City with their white women on their arms. Most of the wives knew of their practices, because every now and again, they came over to the house. While the men were outside manning the barbecue grill and exchanging one dramatic lie with another, the women gathered at the kitchen table, exchanging ideas on the whereabouts of their spouses on certain Sundays. Mommy was the listener who rarely gave input. She never knew if word would get back to him that she was questioning his whereabouts. If it did, she knew what the damaging results would be.

There was one good side to the Masons. When he was out late at some lodge meeting in New York City or not coming home at night at all, Mommy let us stay up late and eat potato chips and ice cream while she rested in bed. I loved to lay across the bed, resting my head on her stomach. Robert would lay at her feet. Those were the best nights of all.

CHAPTER 11

Mathematics

Whack! Whack! Whack!

The whistling sound of the wind was sharp and quick as the wooden ruler came crashing down across my knuckles. The sharp, stinging pain shot from my fingertips up my right arm.

"Look at it this! Does that look right to you? Look at it!" With his knees slightly bent, my father leaned over and yelled into my left ear. "You better look at it and look at it good, because you only have one more muthafuckin' chance to get it right before I knock you the fuck out of this chair!"

I squeezed my butt and thighs, so the pee did not run down my legs.

"What isssss…thirty-eight times twelve?"

The shrill voice made my insides run cold and my body shake. The intensive heat of his sour breath on my face made me fear I would lose my bowels. As I clenched my buttocks tighter together, I tried to psyche myself out. I was more focused on not peeing on myself than getting the right answer. I had to hold it, push the pee back up. My soul was trying to overcome my will to want to go. There was no way I could concentrate on coming up with the answer in the split second he had allotted me. I could barely write one number under the intensity of his cursing wrath.

It was seven o'clock when he ordered me to the kitchen table to do my dreaded math homework, and I had no idea how much time had passed. Minutes? Hours? The intensity of the fluorescent light made me drunk with sleepiness. The pain piercing my bleeding knuckles made it difficult to hold the pencil steady on the loose-leaf paper.

"Girl, you got until the count of three to put the answer on that paper."

His cold, soulless stare was relentless. The heat of the light brought sweat, pouring down over his bushy, black, scraggly eyebrows. The sourness of his breath against my cheek made the contents of my gut bubble up. My bowels begin to weaken. The will of my soul fought to keep the pencil from falling out of my numb hands. *Why won't this pencil write any faster*, I thought. *Two times eight is sixteen, put down the six, and carry the……*

Whack! Whack! Whack!

I felt the ruler connect on my knuckles twice though he lashed down on them three times. The numbness had settled in my hand.

"I said get it on the paper! Do you think I have all mutha-fuckin' night to be sitting up here with your dumb slow ass?" This time we were nose to nose. His bloodshot stare down made my eyes cross.

I tried to control my bottom lip from quivering but failed. I was too scared to cry. Trickling streams of pee had escaped, making their way down my legs, slowly soaking into my slouched white socks. I was never good at con-trolling all my bodily functions at once under extreme pressure and fear.

"I smell something! What the—" His voice trailed off. "Are you pissing on yourself?" he screamed in my face.

"No, sir," I said as my spirit began to pray.

"I smell piss!" he barked as he began sniffing around my personal space. "Girllllllllll! If you peed on yourself, I will bust you in your muthafuckin' face." As he turned his head to call for Robert, I quickly uncrossed my legs and rubbed them together so that they could dry and then recrossed them. "Wendy, get that boy out of the bed and bring his ass here!"

Mommy had been on the couch grading her students' typing assignments for the last hour.

"Hurry up. If he is asleep, wake his little ass up!"

The deep creases that had settled into Robert's navy-blue cotton pajamas with white piping was a clear indication that he had been in a deep sleep for some time. Rubbing his eyes to wake himself up, he slowly stumbled down the hall. "Yes, sir?"

"What is thirty-eight times twelve?" His commands resembled those of a Marine drill sergeant.

"Well, errrrrr, ugh, it is a…"

"Sit the fuck down there, and show your dumb ass sister."

Before Robert knew it, he pushed him so hard into the chair that he had to catch himself to keep from falling out.

"Welllll, pick up the pencil, stupid!" he yelled as he pointed at the blood-smeared number 2 pencil on the kitchen table in front of me. "I tell you, you are as much a dumb ass as her! Between the two of you, you better figure it the fuck out." Abruptly, he rose from the chair next to me. I almost jumped out of my seat with fear. "What the fuck are you jumping for? I have not given you nothing to jump for yet. Wendy, where is my cup? Pour me a drink! I see these little muthafuckers gonna have me up all goddamn night!" He stomped off into the living room and plopped onto the beige-and-brown suede sectional sofa. He sat on the end so that he could be closer to the kitchen.

Unbeknown to me, my right hand was still clenched. Robert pointed the eraser of the pencil toward my hand. As I slowly looked down, two streams of blood were making their way down my knuckles. Quickly, I brushed my left hand over my knuckles before the blood hit the loose-leaf paper. The numbness kept me from feeling the touch of the eraser. The blood temporarily stopped, but the sight of the white bones of my knuckles peering through my slashed, bloodied, broken skin made me want to vomit.

Mommy came into the kitchen to retrieve a glass from the cabinet. Slowly, I raised my head. She was mouthing something that I could not decipher no matter my desperate attempt to read her lips while trying not to let him see that I was attempting eye contact. At times, I thought he had eyes in the back of his head.

"C'mon, girl. You're slow." His bark caught me off guard, and I jumped in my pee-stained seat.

"What did you do with your glass? I can't find it," Mommy lied.

"Well, then get me a clean one!" he shouted. "Damn! Now I know where these dumb asses get their damn brains from. Just bring me another glass with some ice in it!"

The insults cut like a knife, but they were a lesser evil than a beating. Mommy was stalling until she could get the answer to me and I could get it to Robert before he caught on. She came over to the refrigerator and looked over her left shoulder into the family room to see if he was looking. Luckily, he was not. In the blink of an eye, she leaned down and whispered in Robert's ear as she opened the freezer door. The clink of the ice cubes in the glass was sharp and swift. She closed the door quickly and exited the kitchen.

Robert quickly scribbled something on the paper.

I heard the squish of the living room sofa as he rose off the couch to make his way back to the kitchen. His feet hit the hardwood floor. "Let me see what you've got." He was standing in my personal space, looking over the top of my head. A black streak came across the paper as my father ripped it away from under the pencil while Robert was still writing.

"Four hundred and fifty-six," Robert said.

"Well, it's about fuckin' time," he said as he shoved the paper across the table. It landed in Robert's lap. "Finish the rest of these problems, and show stupid over here how you come up with the answers." The spit from his lips landed on my face. "You're gonna learn to do this here math if it kills you. When you are done, have your mother check it. Wendy, if there are any problems wrong after you check it, I am gonna lay into your dumb ass. This is your fault why these chillen are so muthafuckin' stupid. Do you hear me?"

"Yes, Robert. I hear you," she said in an obedient tone.

He stormed off to their bedroom and slammed the door. I relaxed my legs and let the pee flow freely down into my white bobby socks.

Later, Mommy cried through her prayers as she gently, quietly wrapped my injured hand. I gazed at the medium-sized, beige Tupperware bowl with cubes of ice and crimson-colored water.

I whispered through my pain, "Don't cry, Mommy. It will be all right. God's gonna get him, and I'm gonna practice my math really hard."

CHAPTER 12

Brother's Keeper

Despite our pact that we would stick together and never leave one behind, Mommy told Robert and me that we had to go to college and never look back. She said not to worry about her. She would find us when the time was right.

Robert was the first to go. He was my constant companion, playmate, friend, co-conspirator—my protector. He was the man of the house whenever the devil father was not home, and he took his position seriously.

In the summer of 1984, he left for the University of Maryland Eastern Shore (UMES). He did not want to leave us, and he did not want to go to UMES. UMES was the alma mater of the devil. He said he had relatives who worked there and would keep an eye on Robert and report daily with their findings. Robert would not be able to breathe with my father's lurking spies.

I tried to put up a brave face when the day came. We drove the five hours to Princess Anne, Maryland, to move Robert into his new home. Silently, part of me died inside. Robert and I had the normal sister and brother arguments, but he was my everything. He did not just protect me from my father. He kept me in line when we were at school, because my quick temper sometimes made it difficult to keep me off someone's ass for saying something disrespectful or trying to bully me. It did not matter whether it was a girl or a boy—I was ready to fight at a moment's notice. From elementary to high school, it was not uncommon for some white kid to call us niggers. I could tell it bothered Robert, because he stared down the kid and clenched his teeth with a stern look, eyes fixed on them like he wanted to unload on them. He held back because he knew he could beat the shit out of them and hurt them bad. I, on the other hand, was a bully and would kick ass and ask questions later. I did not fight every day, but the fights I had were legendary.

I remember one fight in particular. All the kids were bundled up tight in full or waist-length wool coats, hats, scarves, and gloves or mittens, standing on the corner while waiting for the school bus. The Long Island winters were raw, so it would have been challenging had it not been for the snowball fights. Running around was what kept us warm.

Finally, the bus made its way down Manatuck Boulevard, and everyone boarded. The hissing of the door opening when it stopped at the next corner was deafening. The busy chatter ceased. The winter wind swiftly ushered in the odor of rotten eggs. When Miguel Gonzalez boarded, some of the kids made no eye contact, while most pulled up their scarves or coats to shield themselves from the odor. His dirty, brown hair was matted, and the oily, scraggly strands fell to his shoulders. His dingy, brown complexion was marred with coal-colored spots all over his face. You knew if you spit on a Kleenex and brushed his face, it would wipe off. His oversized, dingy, green winter parka was hanging off his body. His ill-fitting, faded jeans looked as if they had been wiped on the floor of an automotive garage, and the knees were soiled with holes. His snow-soaked cloth sneakers had muddy, tattered laces too short to feed into all the eyelets.

He came to the back of the bus. He plopped down on the lap of the person in the back seat and laughed when they pushed him off and ran down the aisle to another seat. His rancid odor was like a sewer.

The bus started down the street. Not ten minutes into the ride, a ball of paper landed in front of our seat, hitting a girl in the head. "Hey, slut, throw it back!"

The girl picked up the ball and threw it to the back of the bus. "Stop it, Miguel," she said in protest.

"Shut up, slut. Why don't you come back here and make me?"

The next paper ball landed in our seat, and Robert flicked it onto the floor.

"Hey, nigga, throw it back."

The third paper ricocheted off the top of Robert's toboggan hat and landed two seats in front of us. "Hey, nigga, you deaf? Throw it back."

I eased my right foot halfway into the aisle.

"Sis, ignore his dirty ass," Robert said.

We were blocks away from West Junior High School.

The ripping sound of notebook paper being torn from a spiral notebook sent a hot surge through my body. I pressed my left palm on the green leather seat. The crushing sound of his balling up the paper sent my psyche to a point of no return. The soreness in my leg from being thrown to the floor the night before due to a C grade in math came back to me as I pressed my right foot down in the aisle.

The fourth paper ball hit Robert in the head.

Quickly, I threw all of my weight to my right leg and shot it into the aisle like Flo Jo pushing off the starting blocks of the hundred-meter dash. I leapt onto the seat behind me and used the lap of the kid in the seat to push off as I lunged my body over two seats. Hands stretched out, I grabbed handfuls of his dirty, oily hair, snatching him toward me.

"Get him! Get him! Get him!" Shouts roared from the kids on the bus.

The sourness of his rancid breath that reeked of spoiled milk turned my stomach. I pummeled his head with my right fist while my left hand was slipping from the oiliness of his hair.

"Bitch, get off me!" he screamed.

"Sis, let go!" Robert grabbed the back of my coat, attempting to pull me back.

I continued pummeling his head. When my left hand slipped down his hair, I grabbed his snorkel hood and pulled it over his head as I kept banging it on and off the top of the seat. The momentum of the abrupt stop of the bus pushed me into his face.

"You fucken' bitch, get off me!"

I wanted to shut him up. With my left hand, I pulled him up and toward me and slammed his head against the window above the back of his seat. With my right hand, I attempted to zip his snorkel hood closed over his head, but it kept getting stuck. Furiously, I unzipped and zipped it up harder each time, but it kept getting stuck halfway. His eyes dulled and were rolling back in his head. Someone was pulling on my ankles.

"Get off my sister! Get off my sister!" Robert roared. "Sister, let go! Let go!"

I yanked the zipper up and down, up and down, and it kept getting stuck. Robert's arms were wrapped around my waist. His head was buried in my back. Miguel's body went limp as I continued to slam his head against the seat.

Robert yanked me one last time, and the force pushed us both into the seat.

"Everybody get back in their damn seats NOW!" The driver pointed his finger in our faces. "You and you get to the front of the bus!"

I got off Robert, and some of the kids handed us our book bags.

"Is he dead?" someone asked behind me as I walked up the aisle. "Yeah! Yeah!" the students cheered.

The guidance counselor called Grandma Spencer, since she was our emergency contact, and she drove to the school to pick me up. They sent Robert to class.

"Wendy, what happened? Why were you fighting on the bus? You know you shouldn't be fighting."

"Grandma, it was that dirty filthy Miguel Gonzalez. He is always coming on the bus and messing with people. He was throwing paper and called Robert a bad word."

"What did he call him?"

"A nigga."

"Well, you know you should have ignored him. You know that boy is mean spirited." She drove me back to her house. "I have your schoolwork for today, so when we get home, you will sit down and do it. I need you to change out of those clothes so they can be washed and pressed."

I ate, did my schoolwork, and sat in the living room wondering what Robert was doing. By three o'clock, the front door slammed. It was Robert. "Hey, sis, you okay?" He smiled.

"Yes."

"Sis, everyone at school was asking where you were."

Robert did his homework, Grandma gave us a snack, and we watched TV.

"Wendy and Robert, Mrs. Howell called and said she had a meeting after school so she will be here later to pick you up."

Later that afternoon, one of Grandma Spencer's older daughters, Carol, arrived home from work. "Hey, Wendy and Robert. What's happening? How was school?"

Before either of us could answer, Grandma Spencer did, "Wendy got into a fight on the bus, and the school called me to come sign her out and pick her up."

"Did you win?" Carol said.

"Carol, it's not funny!" Grandma Spencer shouted from the kitchen.

Carol sat next to me on the couch and whispered, "Who were you in a fight with, Wendy?"

"Miguel Gonzalez."

"Who is that?"

"He is a little dirty boy who hardly ever comes to school, and when he does, he bullies people. He steals peoples' lunches and beats them up for their lunch money."

"Did you win?"

"Yeah, she choked him and beat him in the back of the bus," Robert said.

"Carol!" Grandma Spencer yelled.

It was early evening, and everyone was eating dinner when a knock came at the front door. Grandma Spencer got up to answer. A woman with a thick Spanish accent said, "Hello, I would like to speak with Mrs. Howell."

"Who may I ask are you?" Grandma Spencer asked with perfect diction.

"I am Miguel Gonzalez's mother, and this is my son, Miguel. Wendy did this to my son." The woman pointed to deep, black-and-blue zipper marks with missing chunks of skin in the crevasses of his neck. The thick, black threading did nothing to cover it up.

Carol got up from the dinner table and headed to the door. She was average height with beautiful black hair, soft, dark-brown eyes, a flawless pecan skin tone, full lips, and a small waist. She had perfect diction and commuted daily to New York City for her work as an accountant. She stood next to Grandma Spencer in the doorway. "How can I help you?"

Miguel's mother spoke louder. "Your daughter did this to my son!"

"What did your son do to Wendy?" Carol asked with an inquisitive tone.

"It doesn't matter what he did to her. He did not deserve this. Look at his neck. He has burns, and his skin is missing! I want to know who is going to pay his doctor bills. He had to have stitches to close his neck up!"

Carol asked her to lower her voice, and that seemed to incite her. "Your daughter did this to my son!"

"Mommy, excuse me." Carol gently moved Grandma Spencer to the side and stood in front of her. The tone of her voice rose. "First of all, I do not appreciate you raising your voice toward my mother. I asked you to lower your voice, and I'm not going to ask you one more time." Carol was the nonviolent type and did not look for trouble, but when it came to her family, she was a fierce lioness.

Miguel's mother grew angrier. "Your daughter is an animal, and I am going to call the police."

Carol snapped, "You think your son's ass got beat? Well, if you do not get away from my door, I am going to beat your ass worse than she beat his, and you're gonna wish you never came to my door. Now I suggest you get your ass away from my door!"

"I am going to call the police! Your daughter should be locked away!" Miguel's mother yelled.

"Call the police, and I will tell them how you came to my house threatening me. Now get out of here unless you want your ass beat worse than your filthy kid!" Carol slammed the door and locked it. "Mommy, I am sorry you had to hear that, but can you believe that woman? Everyone knows what a bully her son is. Wendy, stay away from that boy in school."

She sat down, and we finished our dinner. I smiled at Robert, and he shook his head.

Now, he was off to college, and I was on my own with Mommy—and him.

CHAPTER 13

Saboteur

My grandmother—my father's mother—had a slight hump in her back. If she stood up straight, she was about five feet three. She was a mulatto: her mother was white and her father black, so her complexion was very fair. Her stringy, mixed-gray hair was usually worn in a slightly disheveled pageboy. The way her sneaky eyes peered over her rectangle glasses made you feel as though she was always spying on you. Robert, Mommy, and I hated going to visit her.

My father bragged to his friends and lodge brothers that he grew up on a large working farm and in a beautiful home. Nothing could be further from the truth.

The half-mile dirt driveway led to an old, gray, two-story home that resembled a haunted house. The front porch's cracked, prison-gray floorboards squeaked and sank when you walked on them. I hated walking on them because I knew it was a matter of time before the floor would give way. My only hope would be that it would be him that fell through the floor instead of Mommy, Robert, or me. All the windows had cracked white trim, some in such disrepair that you could see where the paint fell off, exposing the warped wood frame. A bird had built its nest in the porch roof. At night, you could hear squirrels, raccoons, and other small animals running around the ceiling. An old, gray, dirty, dusty pickup truck was in the front yard. A broken-down red truck, resembling Fred the Junk Man's on the TV show *Sanford and Son*, was in the garage.

Acres of field stretched as far as the eye could see on both sides of the haunted house. Depending on the season, the fields had full rows and rows of watermelons, cantaloupes, corn, and cucumbers. Now, they sat untended. Two tall, weather-beaten stakes held a clothesline where gray or green work pants had hung. Old, green lawn chairs were scattered in the dusty driveway.

Worst of all was not how rundown the house was but how emotionally cold and uneasy it was inside.

As my father's father grew older and my grandmother could no longer care for him, my father decided to place him in a nursing home. My grandmother remained in her home. However, whenever we went to visit once a month and on holidays, he thought she was not taking care of herself or the house. After a few years of her living alone, he decided to move her to Long Island with us, a decision she was strongly against. After a life of abuse from her husband, she liked to be alone and was at peace for once.

When she came to live with us, I thought that maybe with her in our house, he would not beat on us as much, because she would be watching and listening. I thought he would be too embarrassed to allow her to see how he abused us. I found out that was not to be, because he also hit her. To make things worse, she lied, saying she had not eaten all day because Mommy would not let her in her kitchen, which was of course a lie. I suppose she thought she could deflect her beatings to us, since she was outside our pact of protection. I suppose she thought she could be on his side. There was no room for her there, only for him.

She stayed in her bedroom. After everyone else was up and getting breakfast, someone had to go and get her. She acted as if she was just waking up, but we could hear her walking around in her room while we ate in the kitchen.

In normal situations, grandparents are the ones who stand up for the grandchildren, spoil them, and protect them. This was not a normal situation by any means. She did not like living with us and preferred her run-down farm home in Salisbury. There she had the freedom to come and go as she wanted, and with her abusive husband in a nursing home, she was finally free. She went to visit him whenever she liked, which was not often, and no one could tell her to do anything different. The townspeople and relatives told stories that her husband used to brutally physically and verbally abuse her and her children. That would answer the question of why we were victims of the same. When she came to live with us, she went right back to her old life, only now, it was her son who beat her.

"Wendy, is my dinner ready? Where you at?"

Mommy and I were sitting at the kitchen table, eating dinner. The place setting next to me had not been used. "Robert, we are in here," Mom said.

He stomped into the kitchen, demanding his dinner. His TV tray was already set up in the family room in front of the television. Mommy rose to turn the burners on under the pots to warm the broccoli, mashed potatoes, and gravy. The meatloaf was warming in the oven.

"Well, make me a plate. Where's Momma? Did you call her to eat?"

"Yes, Robert. I called her twice, and Wendy went to her room to call her for dinner."

"Mama!"

The sound of his deliberate stomps through the living room, making his way to her room, were all too familiar. Quickly, I pushed the last two bites of meatloaf and mashed potatoes onto my fork with my fingers.

"Mama, did Wendy call you to eat? Wendy, get in here!"

Mommy exited the kitchen and started walking toward the living room.

"Not you!"

I quickly filled his Styrofoam cup with ice, placed it on the countertop, and headed to her room. "Did you call your grandmother to dinner?"

"Yes."

He gripped my grandmother up by her left arm and shook her.

"Robert, that's my arm!" she protested.

"Wendy, get back to the table!"

Quickly, I made my way back to the kitchen. The dull thud of the bedroom floor shook me.

Mommy had filled his plate, and it was waiting for him on his TV tray. His deliberate stomps were too close for comfort. "Wendy, what the hell are you doing?"

Again with the questions, I thought. *You see this broom in my hand. What do you think I am doing?* Clearly, he could see I was doing my chore of sweeping the kitchen floor after dinner. "I'm—"

"Put that damn broom away, and leave the kitchen." He stomped into the family room and plopped down in his chair. "I work all day. I don't need to come home to this shit!" he roared.

I swept up the small pile of crumbs into the dustpan and returned the broom and dustpan to the kitchen closet. As I walked out of the kitchen, his mother was slowly limping out of her bedroom, her hair angrily tousled all over her head like a mad scientist. She held her left arm. I brushed past her without making eye contact and retreated to my room.

CHAPTER 14

UMES

loved Spanish class. Today, my happiness was interrupted by a knock at the door. Mrs. Johnston, the principal's secretary, peered through the window.

"Pardon me, estudiantes." My teacher, Mrs. Rodriguez, opened the door and slowly closed it behind her. The pit of my stomach went empty and cold. The longer they talked, the more fearful I became. *What happened to Mommy? Did he kill her? Is she in the hospital?* This was not looking good.

"Senorita Wendy, por favor?" She motioned me forward with a look of concern. I squeezed my vagina, hoping pee would not begin to run down my leg. I slowly got up from the desk and made my way out of the classroom. I swallowed the frog in my throat and leaned into her arms, trying to prepare for the worst.

Mrs. Johnston placed her arm around my shoulder and spoke in her soft, calm voice. "Wendy, dear, your mother is waiting for you downstairs."

Total relief. Anything beyond this I could handle.

UMES had called. Junior was missing. A week had passed before they figured out that he wasn't on campus. School officials, my father's relatives, and the security team had questioned Junior's roommate and were not able to determine where he was. My grandparents in Laurel were called and questioned, but they had not heard from him.

I was relieved to see Mommy downstairs outside the front office, waiting for me. "Baby, do you have all of your stuff so we can leave?"

"No, Mom, I need to go to my locker."

"Okay, well, quickly grab your stuff so we can go. He is waiting in the car. Do you need me to come with you?"

"No, Mom. I will be right back."

I raced upstairs and ran down the hallway to my locker. I spun the dial on the combination, yanked the door open, dumped my books into my book bag, threw my jacket over my shoulder, and ran back downstairs.

Mommy spoke quickly. "Wendy, Junior finally left school, and when I last spoke to Mom, he was on his way to basic training and said he would reach out once he arrived. He said after that, it would be a few months until he would be allowed to make contact. Your father is furious, and we are on our way to Maryland. He has it in his mind that he is going to threaten his roommate to tell where he is. Robert told your grandmother that his roommate is solid and will not tell where he is, even under pressure. If he asks, you know nothing, you got it?"

Mommy did not have to tell me twice. He could beat me from New York to Maryland and back. There was no way that I would give up Robert.

CHAPTER 15

South Shore

Part of the athletic director's job was to oversee all sporting events for Nassau County, including on weekends. We loved Saturdays, because it was the one day of the week we could be normal kids. With him out of the house for hours, our guard came down. We did not have the fear of looking over our shoulders, wondering which one of us would be his next target. Our chores had to be completed first, but they were always done early.

Just knowing that he was not around to snatch us up for not doing something to his specifications, or cursing us or Mommy out, was enough, but she always had something fun planned for us to do. Usually, if he had a lot of events to oversee, he did not come back until early evening, so we got to stay out longer with Mommy. We would get pizza, burgers, Chinese food, or KFC for dinner and ice cream from Carvel. The world was our oyster on Saturdays.

After breakfast, I loaded the dishwasher. This was another treat for me, because he forbade us to use the dishwasher. He said it wasted too much water, and since his mother never had a dishwasher when he grew up, we were not going to use one. Well, we used it on Saturdays. While the dishwasher was running, it freed Mommy and me to do the other chores. "Baby, make sure you grab all your dirty clothes out of your room. Make sure there is nothing left on your closet floor. Strip your bed. Don't forget your gym suit and sneakers."

I loved gym class, but I hated that damn one-piece gym suit. Mom said, "Never use the word hate. If you do not like something, just say you dislike it." She was always teaching even when she was not in the classroom. Sorry, Mom, but I hated that gym suit. It was a one-piece short set that snapped down the front with metal circles. It had an elastic waist and elastic around the legs, which gave it an awful, oversized, puffy look. I had a white one and a navy-blue one and did not know which one was worse. Neither one was flattering. When I wore it, I rolled up the sleeves and popped the collar so that maybe I looked a little cool. I asked Mommy to starch the collar and sleeves so they could stick up and out. The white knit knee-high gym socks with two black bands around the top did not help my cool quotient. The only good thing about it was that it was a regulated suit, so all the girls had to wear them. The boys would hurry and get changed into their shorts and T-shirts so they could glare at us as we exited the locker room.

After balling everything up into the sheets, I ran across the hall into the master bathroom. I emptied the dirty clothes out of the wicker clothes hamper into a large clothes basket and returned to the kitchen.

"Are you sure you have everything?" Mommy gave the load a close look.

"Yup," I said.

She grabbed the load and headed downstairs to load it into the washing machine. I went to the utility closet in the kitchen and grabbed the Lemon Pledge and an old T-shirt that served as a dust rag. I quickly dusted the furniture in the family room and dining room.

Mommy came upstairs, retrieved the dust mop and the Kirby vacuum cleaner from the closet, and headed for the family room. "Baby, spray some of that polish on the mop for Mommy." She held the mop up for me, and after I sprayed it, she began to dust the floor.

"I'll start the vacuum."

"No, no. After you sweep the kitchen floor, you can gather the coupons and begin making the grocery list."

"All right, Mom, but while you are dusting the floor, I can vacuum."

"No, no. That vacuum is too heavy for you to lift, and I do not want you to hurt yourself. Please do as I say." Her voice was a bit firmer.

"Okay, Mom. I was just trying to help."

"I know, and thank you. You are a big help to Mommy already. Just do as I say so we can hurry up and get out of here before he comes back. You do want to go to the mall, don't you?"

"Yes," I said with great enthusiasm.

"Okay, well, you need to finish what Mommy asked you to do."

I went to the kitchen and made quick work of the floor, which took all of five minutes. It was rarely dirty, because I swept it every night after dinner and Mommy mopped and waxed it every two weeks. I grabbed the small accordion file of coupons out of the kitchen drawer. I also grabbed the Sunday *Newsday*, a piece of paper, a pen, and a pair of scissors and sat at the kitchen table. I pulled the coupon inserts out of the newspaper. I began flipping through it, looking for things we needed, and circled a few that we could purchase depending on how much money Mommy had left over.

After vacuuming, Mommy sat at the table. "We need milk, bread, a dozen eggs, Vienna sausage, tuna fish, coffee, sage sausage, cold cuts, and soda. Check the pantry and see what else we need."

Our pantry was enormous. It was solid oak, double-doored from floor to ceiling. You had to stand in a chair to get to the top of the four long shelves. Sometimes when he was not home, my brother hid in there in the dark and then called my name. When I went searching through the fifteen-room house and ended up in the kitchen, he would swing the doors open to scare me. I peed on myself every time. It was great fun. He would hold me in his arms and wipe my tears away while we laughed.

Now, in the twelfth grade, I wished he was home, but he was away at college. I missed him desperately.

I loved making the shopping list and searching for coupons to be used. I loved adding the coupons up in anticipation of how much money we would save at checkout. After selecting the ones we needed, I could select a few for fun stuff like frozen pizza and ice pops. I was allowed to get those extras only if we had enough money left over.

We headed out to South Shore Mall after the grocery shopping was complete. I loved going to the mall on Saturdays, as I hoped to see some of the cool kids from school. He never allowed my brother or me to go out with any of our friends for whatever stupid reason, but Mommy found a way around that obstacle when she could. If she knew she had to go to the mall, she let us know, and I would find out if any of the cool kids were going that weekend. The answer was always yes. They went every weekend. After our chores were completed, my mother took my brother and me. When we saw our friends, she allowed us to go off with them to the arcade, Friendly's, or just walk around while she went browsing in JCPenney. Sometimes she sat in the car to catch up on sleep. She always reminded us that we had only an hour. He timed us wherever we went, so we needed to be home before he got suspicious and came looking for us.

This Saturday, I was meeting Lee, his best friend, Norman, and Norman's girlfriend. We were supposed to be double dating. I kept checking my watch. Lee said they would be there at one o'clock. It was going on one thirty, and they had not shown up. I was getting nervous. I had thirty minutes left before I had to leave. I went out to the car to see if Mommy was there. She was slouched back in the driver's seat, asleep. I lightly tapped on the window so as not to startle her too much, and she awoke immediately. "They are not here yet," I said.

"Well, it is one thirty," she said.

"I know." I had tears in my eyes.

"Well, Wendy, you may just have to see him in school on Monday, because we are going to have to go soon."

The look of sorrow in her eyes made me feel even worse. This was one of the few times I could go on a halfway date, and he was late. I am sure there was a good reason. It was not his fault that my father was such a ferocious dictator that he did not allow my brother or me out with friends. My stomach started bubbling with nerves.

A horn beeped. There was Lee's army-green Dodge.

I looked at my watch. It was one forty-five, only fifteen minutes left. My heart sunk to the pit of my stomach. I ran over to his car. "Hey, I thought you were going to be here at one o'clock."

Lee gave me an embarrassed look. "I'm sorry. Norman had to do something for his mother. Is that your mother over there?" He pointed past my shoulder.

"Yes. We have been here since one o'clock. I only have an hour."

"Well, we wanted to go to Friendly's to get something to eat and then check out a movie. Can't your mom come back for you?"

I guess he temporarily forgot that his girlfriend was not living in a real world. "Lee, we do not know how long we have. We don't know where he is, and we can't take any chances. You know that."

Lee grabbed my hand as I desperately looked into his eyes. Sometimes I wished that we could run away together. We often talked about how after graduation, I could move into his house with him, his sister, and his mother. Of course, that would not work, because my father would come looking for me, and when he found me, it would be curtains for Lee and me. However, Lee was brave. He said he was not scared of him and that if he came to his house, he would call the police. Lee said I would be eighteen by then, and he could no longer put his hands on me. If he did, he would get the police after him.

Little did he know that the man feared no one. Anyway, I would never leave Mommy behind.

"Let me ask your mom if you can stay longer." Lee grabbed my hand and walked me over to Mommy's Buick Riviera. "Hey, Mrs. Howell, how are you today?" His smile was easy and debilitating.

"Well, hello Lee," she said in a sweet, lovely tone. She loved Lee. He was sweet to me, treated me nicely, was well-mannered, respectful of me and Mommy, and did well in school. He had risen as the man in his house since his parents divorced and his father moved to Brooklyn and remarried. In addition, his mother was a nice Christian woman, and Mommy admired her for raising two children single-handedly.

"Mrs. Howell, I was wondering if Wendy could go with us to Friendly's. We were going to take in a movie afterward."

"Well, baby, Wendy has to leave right now. Maybe some other time."

I was devastated. I wanted to walk hand in hand with him in the mall like the other couples.

"Is there any way that you have something to do and can come back for her?" Lee begged her to change her mind. He understood what we were up against. However, what I loved about him was that he always wanted to protect me. I felt that as long as I was in his care, I would be okay. The confidence of his love melted my heart, so I was willing to take the chance.

"Wendy, you know we only have an hour, and we are taking a chance being here and someone seeing you with Lee. Some other time." Her words were final.

"Mommy, pleassssse, pleassssse?" I begged as if my life depended on that moment. I knew what we were risking. I hoped that something extraordinary could be done. I was begging for a miracle.

"Wellll, I have to go to the farmers market to get some vegetables. I will be back in one hour, Wendy, and I mean it. One hour, and you better be out here." Her voice trembled because she knew what we were both risking, and she was taking that risk for me.

"Thank you, Mommy, thank you." I leaned into the window and placed a long kiss on her cheek.

"Thank you, Mrs. Howell."

"Lee, please have her out here in an hour."

"Mrs. Howell, my word is bond." He reached in the window and lightly touched the top of her shoulder.

"Okay, so what do you want to do?" I asked, turning to look at Lee.

"We can go to Friendly's. We're not going to be able to see the movie." He sounded slightly disappointed.

I do not know how Lee put up with me throughout senior year. He could have dated any of the girls who lined up to be with the star quarterback, but he chose me. He knew what he had to go through to see me, and he told me over and over that he did not care. He did not blame me for the way my father treated me. Oftentimes, Lee spoke of getting someone to deal with him. He did not approve of a man hitting on a girl and her mom. He didn't understand why we couldn't leave no matter how many times I explained how he threatened us if we did and threatened Mommy's mother and father.

"Let's go to Friendly's. It'll be fun." My attempt to refocus him worked. We talked endlessly about the prom, what colors we were wearing, what color the limo was going to be, and the after-prom. Time flew by, and it was time to go.

"Okay, let's go. I promised your mom I would have you back," Lee said.

As we walked through the mall hand in hand, I hoped we would run into some kids from school. Kids never understood why they never saw my brother or me hanging out at the local spots in town. If someone saw me today, that would dispel the rumors going around that we were never allowed out.

Thank goodness this was our little secret, and my father never found out about our date.

CHAPTER 16

UMES 2.0

swallowed deeply as I approached the car, careful not to look away from his stare.

"Wendy, we on our way to Maryland. That dumb brother of yours cannot be found on campus. You know anything about it?" The interrogating stare he gave me from the rearview mirror did not move me.

"Where is Robert?" I pleaded.

"That's what I'm asking you."

"No, I have not heard from Robert." I lied as I looked directly at his stoic stare, glaring at me from the rearview mirror.

"Well, I asked your Mammy over here, and she said she ain't heard from him either. Mighty funny, I called those damn grandparents of yours, and everybody saying the same damn thing. I know one muthafuckin' thing. If I hear that any of you muthafuckers know anything about this, you will regret you ever lied to me. Do you hear me?"

I jumped in the back seat slightly as he grabbed a handful of Mommy's hair from the back, shook her, and sped out of the Sonderling High parking lot.

We drove straight through to UMES in silence. As we approached the entrance to the university, he broke the deafening five-hour silence. "As soon as I get in that room, that boy better tell me where his dumb ass is, 'cause he know. Wendy, stay your ass in the car. Your mother and I will go in."

Mommy shared with me that they first went to a classroom to meet one of the relatives who called to advise us of Junior's disappearance. He said they had questioned the roommate, but he was not giving up anything. My stomach was bubbling with nerves. I knew Robert was far away, but I was terrified that his roommate would break under pressure, and if he did, I didn't know what my father would do to Mommy and me.

The wait seemed like hours. The sun had just gone down when I heard voices nearby. I was too afraid to turn around to see who it was. The car door opened, and Mommy got in and spoke quickly. "Wendy, the roommate did not say anything even though your father threatened to beat him."

"Mom, where are we going now?"

"To the house, I guess. Be quiet. Here he comes."

He got in the car and slammed the door so hard the car shook. There was a man standing outside the car window.

"Robert, we gonna have another crack at that boy tomorrow morning. We catch him early, so he won't be expecting us. In the meantime, I'm going to ask around campus if someone knows something."

"Okay, Cecil. I appreciate it. We gonna be back here tomorrow, and if I have to beat it out of him, that boy is going to talk. He knows where Robert is hiding."

"Well now, Robert, come get me when you arrive tomorrow. I don't want you going over there by yourself. We gotta be careful."

"Cecil, I don't give a damn. He gonna know who Robert Howell the fuck is when I get back here tomorrow."

"Robert, you have to tread lightly. That's why I said come and get me when you arrive to question that boy again so we can go together."

"Okay, Cecil. We gonna play it your way, but I ain't got all day. That boy is gonna tell me something tomorrow, or I'm gonna have to ask you to step outside the room and leave me with him for a few minutes. I will get it out of him then. Well, I gotta get these two to the house so we can get something to eat. I will see you tomorrow." He said to Mommy, "Wendy, I don't need your ass in there tomorrow. This is man's business."

On the way, we stopped to get three individual two-piece fried chicken, biscuit, and fries meals from a gas station in town and then headed to his parents' house for the night.

"Wendy, get in there. Eat and wash up and go to bed. We getting up early tomorrow to head on back to that school and then back up the road to New York."

I lay awake all night, wondering where Robert was and what he was doing. I was glad he had escaped to the military but was sad that I did not get a chance to talk to him before he left. Mom Mom Hamilton said he would call or write her once he was settled in basic training camp to let her know he was okay.

The next morning, Mommy came into the room. "Wendy, are you awake?"

I must have dozed off during the night for a catnap. My eyes quickly opened.

"Look, he is downstairs in the shower. Get up and get your clothes ready, and I will let you know when he is out."

"Mom, what happened yesterday?" I was so anxious to know.

"He went in there with that cousin of his and threatened Robert's roommate. That poor child was so scared, the fear in his eyes was sad, but he never told where Robert was no matter how much he was being threatened. Your father threatened that if the boy did not tell him where to find Robert, he would come back today and beat it out of him."

"Oh no, Mom, will he tell?" My stomach began to bubble up.

"Wendy, when Robert's roommate called Mom Mom to tell him that Robert had left, he gave his word he would never tell his father where he could locate him. Robert and he are tight, so I believe him. Mom said we may not hear from him for a while since he is in basic training, but she said he sounded relieved to get off of that campus. He was being followed everywhere by your father's cousins. Now get up, and I will call you soon."

I felt relieved that Robert was okay and had been in contact with Mom Mom and Pop Pop Hamilton.

CHAPTER 17

Oorah!

"That girl betta be up and ready or she will be left!" The shouting of his commands would have awakened the dead.

Thankfully, Mommy had eased me out of sleep by gently patting my back asking me to wake up to get in the shower. "Wendy, Wendy, wake up, baby. It's time to get up."

The soothing tone of her voice eased me out of my semi-sleep state. I had awakened earlier after tossing and turning the entire night, wondering what Robert was doing. I was glad he left school.

When he was able to get a call through, he let us know that he and his roommate were constantly followed wherever they went on campus. He said if they went to the café, there was someone there, and the same man would show up at the library, peering at him between the bookcases. A lot of his dorm mates told him and his roommate that the man, who he later learned was a cousin of our father, would knock on their door at night and question them on their whereabouts. The dorm mates all stuck together and never gave them up, but it was embarrassing just the same. Robert said he was late one day to one of his classes, and the next day he saw the cousin peering through the narrow glass window of the class, searching for him. One night, he and his roommate went to a party on campus, and before they left, they told their dorm mates that if the man came, asking for his whereabouts, to send him on a wild goose chase, which they happily did.

"Wendy, wake up so you can get showered and dressed. By the time he is ready, you will be ready," Mommy said.

I got up, showered, and dressed. I couldn't wait to leave. I went downstairs and waited patiently.

Soon Mommy came downstairs to give me the once over. "We will get something to eat on the road. Put your things in the car, and he should be down soon."

Within minutes, we were speeding down the long dirt driveway, kicking up dust everywhere, to reach the main road. "We should be on the road to New York in a few hours. I want to beat traffic on the turnpike," my father said.

As we circled the UMES parking lot, the man we saw yesterday was on the sidewalk, waving his hand and motioning us forward.

"There's Cecil. He better be ready."

We pulled into the parking space, and before he could turn the car off, Cecil was motioning for him to roll the window down. "I asked around and found out that Robert and that roommate of his met with a recruiter from the Marines quite a few times," Cecil said.

"What the hell, the Marines!" my father yelled. "Wendy, do you hear this shit? Your dumb ass son has gone and joined the goddamn Marines."

Cecil continued to snitch. "Yeah, a couple of times a van came to pick them up and take them in town to the recruiting office."

"What the fuck was he meeting with the Marines for? That boy ain't built for no goddamn Marines! Cecil, back up. I'm getting out." He turned the car off and swung the car door open. "Wendy, you wait here, and I will be right back. That goddamn roommate of his will tell me something today if I have to beat it out of him. I do not have time for his shit. We gotta get up the road back to New York, and do not have time for no bullshit." The car shook with the slamming of the door.

"Robert, wait. That kid is not up there," Cecil said.

"Whatchu mean, he is not up there?" He leaned forward, nose to nose with Cecil.

"I mean, I got here early and went up to his room to surprise him, and he was not there." Cecil backed up two steps from my father's sweaty nose.

"Well, where the hell is he?"

"I don't know, and none of those kids in the dorm are talking. I checked the logs, and he has signed out until Tuesday. That's all I know."

"Cecil, you have been no damn help. You told me you would keep an eye on his ass, and you have done a piss poor job."

"Well, err, umm, Robert, I…"

"Cecil, shut up. I have wasted my time with you and coming down here. Shit, you could have saved me a trip and told me this shit over the goddamn phone. I should go down to that recruitment office and punch the shit out of that damn recruiter."

"Robert, it's Sunday, and the office is closed until tomorrow."

"You see what I'm saying? Cecil, you are useless. This is why your dumb ass never left Princess Anne. You can't see past the nose on your stupid ass face. Let's see if you're smart enough to back up or get run over."

He backed the car up fast as if intentionally trying to hit Cecil. The wheels squealed as he sped off the campus.

"Wendy, Imma give you and that dumb ass back there one more chance to tell me if you knew that boy was joining the Marines."

"Robert, I did not know Robert Jr. joined the Marines. Last time he called the house, he only spoke about his classes." Mommy sounded so convincing that I would have believed her had I not known different.

"What about you, dumb ass?" His piercing, bloodshot eyes stared at me in the rearview mirror.

"No, sir. I haven't spoken to Robert."

I always knew the plan. Robert had shared it with Mommy and me several times when he called. He was so weary of being followed and harassed on campus with questions about his whereabouts. He said a recruiter from the US Marines said he and a friend from school could join on the "buddy system." His mind was made up.

It was a way to escape, and escape he did.

CHAPTER 18

The Prom

The senior prom was a rite of passage a girl took on the journey to womanhood. It was an ultimate experience before graduation and said to be like a dress rehearsal for her wedding day. It is supposed to be that special and memorable. I wondered if I would get the chance to take part in that facet of my ever-changing life.

I asked Mommy, "Everyone's talking about the prom. Do you think he would let me go?"

"I don't know, baby. Give me some time, and I'll find a way to approach him about it," Mommy said.

"I really want to go, and tickets are going fast."

"I know you do, and I said I need some time. You know we need to wait until he is drinking, and then he may be in somewhat of a good mood."

"What if I had Lee call and ask? What if I had Lee's mother or father call and ask him? Do you think he would say yes then?"

"I don't know. I'll see. We'll wait a few days and see what Mommy can do, okay?"

Going to the prom would be one of the few things I had in common with my senior friends. They would probably forget that my brother and I did not participate in the parties, sporting events, sleepovers, concerts, mall hangouts, skating, and other cool high school things that he did not allow us to partake in. Prom, I thought, would bring redemption.

My plan was to make sure I did not do anything to make him mad. I would make sure every day that I emptied all the trash cans before he got home, swept the kitchen floor after dinner, and did any other chores assigned to me. I would make sure I was safely tucked away in my room so I would not be a target when he arrived home from school. I would make sure he had his instant coffee in the morning. I found nothing special about scooping out a few spoonfuls of the stuff into a Styrofoam cup with a few spoonfuls of sugar and pouring hot water over it, but he thought it was divine. He said that his baby made his coffee just the way he liked it. Actually, Mommy showed me everything I knew. If this made him happy, and if I knew it would get me closer to the prom and less abusive beatings, I was happy to do it.

I knew that if Mommy said "I'll see," it was almost as good as done, but there was nothing wrong with extra insurance that I might need down the road. A few days passed, and one evening when I was bringing in his tray of dinner, he asked in his fake country slang, "You got a prom coming up, gall, don't cha?"

I hated it when he put on that fake-ass Southern accent, but I played along. "Yes," I said sweetly.

"Well, when were you going to come to the old man about it?"

I shot a glimpse at Mommy sitting on the sofa. She peered over a newspaper with a half hesitant but confident grin on her face. I swallowed deeply and went for it. "Yes, we are having a prom, and Lee asked me if I was going."

"Why didn't he ask your pappy? How much are the tickets? When is it? I ain't seen nothing."

"I have a flyer in my book bag."

"Well, clear these plates away and go get it."

I took his TV tray into the kitchen, cleared his plate, and took the long walk past the family room where he was sitting to retrieve the flyer from my book bag in my room. My hands were shaking, and my throat was dry, but I quickly returned with the flyer. I stood at attention in front of him as he read. I snuck a look over at Mommy, who was faking reading the newspaper while she waited for his response and was just as nervous as me.

"Give this to your mother, and let her read it. Momma, do you remember going to your prom?"

"I don't remember going to mine. I guess I did," she replied with a sly grin.

Who cares if she went to hers, I thought. If it would help me go to mine, I could seem interested.

"Wendy, you better contact that boy's people and find out about this. I wanna know what they are going to do."

"Okay. I'll call them tomorrow."

Without being dismissed, I slowly turned around and went back to my room. I sat on the edge of my bed, unsure of what just occurred, but I had a good feeling like this thing might happen. I quickly undressed, put on my pajamas, and got into bed.

The next day in school, I could not wait to find Lee and tell him the almost good news. We celebrated by cutting class and going to his house next period. I did almost all the talking about what colors we would wear and the limousine selection. Lee had spoken to his buddies on the football team, and two of the guys thought it would be cool to share a limo. They spoke about sneaking alcohol into the limo to drink on the way and, after the prom, going to an all-night diner or some after-prom party. I thought all that would be cool, but I wanted Lee and me to have a limousine all to ourselves. This night was so special to me, and I wanted to share it with only Lee. We could talk about that more at another time. Lee said that financially, sharing would work out for everyone.

Lee's parents were divorced. His father lived in Brooklyn, and Lee and his sister, Cama, lived on Long Island with their mother. Although his father supported Lee and his sister when he could, Lee was being raised by a single parent. His father had another family to raise. Lee's mother worked at a factory and received government assistance. Money was tight, and only the basic necessities were provided, so prom expenses would be a luxury, especially since this was my prom. Lee's prom would be next year. I told him that we would cross that bridge once we got to it, but first we needed to make sure it was going to happen.

That night as I washed the dishes from dinner, Mom called Lee's mother. I knew she was going to say yes, because she was cool and allowed Lee to do anything within reason since he never gave her any trouble. Mom's tone on the phone was light, airy, and personable. When she hung up, I was at her side, waiting for the details.

"Lee's mother will allow Lee to take you to the prom," she said.

Well, that was not a mystery. I knew that, but there seemed to be something else.

"She's financially strapped. She is concerned about their portion of the costs—the tickets, limo, corsage, pictures, and anything else that will come up. She suggested that in lieu of the limo, Lee should drive her car to cut expenses. I told her that since it is your prom, we would pay for the tickets, and they can pay for your corsage. I will get back to her on the rest after I discuss it with your father."

He had not arrived home from school. Mommy saw the look on my face and could tell that I was worried. "Don't worry. Mommy will take care of it. Make sure all your homework is completed. If you have any questions, I will be grading papers in the living room."

I heard his car pull up in the driveway. After all of these years, you would have thought that I was used to hearing his car door slam, but I jumped as if hearing it for the first time. He went into the dining room and then the living room where Mommy sat on the couch, grading papers. He said something to her, but I could not understand it clearly because my door was closed. Sometimes I pressed my ear against my wall to hear sounds from the family room, but this time the television was too loud. When I got up to crack the door, I heard Mommy going into the kitchen. As usual, she was getting his dinner ready. It seemed like hours had passed, and it was time to get ready for bed. I changed into my nightclothes, turned the lights off, and got into bed.

On the drive to school the next morning, I was nervous about what went on after I went to sleep. By the time Mommy reached the end of our block, the silence and suspense were killing me. "What did he say?"

"He never mentioned it. He ate his dinner, drank his vodka, and went to bed."

"You didn't ask him?"

"No. He didn't seem like he was in the mood. I was glad when he went to sleep."

We made our usual stop at the bagel shop for toasted, buttered bagels and orange juice. As I placed our orders, I felt unsure about the whole thing. I returned to the car, pulled my bagel out, and began to eat. The warmth of the butter soothed my insides. I ate in silence as we drove the rest of the way. As we pulled up outside the gates of Sonderling High, she said she loved me, would see me later, and wished me a good day.

I replied with a kiss to her cheek and said the same. I knew that somehow she would make it all right.

CHAPTER 19

Checking In

Every morning without fail, before first period, Lee met me at my locker. That morning, he was not there.

I waited as long as I could until the bell rang for homeroom. I was late to class. I could not concentrate, and my thoughts danced from the prom to Lee. Next period, I saw his best friend, Stacy, who told me that he was at home, sick. Stacy asked me if I was going over to see him after school. I did not want to wait. I wanted to see Lee now.

"Stacy, did you drive today?'

"Yeah. What's up?"

"Can you take me to see Lee after class ends?"

"Of course. Meet me at my locker."

After class, I made my way to his locker and waited. Stacy came down the hallway with a big smile on his face. "I can't leave until after fifth period. I have study hall then. Wait for me in the parking lot."

After fifth period, I made my way out the side door, careful not to be seen by Mrs. Potts or Aunt Mae, who were teacher friends of Mommy and always had their eye out.

On the way to Lee's, Stacy asked about the prom. "So is your pops going to let you go to the prom?"

"I don't know. I hope so. I really want to go."

"Well, I know if you don't, Lee won't mind. "

"He won't mind? What do you mean?"

"I mean, if it was up to Lee, he doesn't care one way or the other. I do not know if he told you or not, but his mom can't really afford it. Lee will have to get the money from his pop or pay for it himself."

"No, he didn't tell me."

"Since this is not his prom, I think he could take it either way. Don't tell him I told you," Stacy said as he pulled up in Lee's driveway. "Tell Lee I'll call him when I get to my girl's house. I'll be back for you in a few hours." When he saw that I was inside, Stacy gave the horn two quick beeps and drove off down the street.

Lee was standing in the doorway in beige pajamas with blue pinstripes. "Hey you." He gently kissed me on my cheek and grasped my left hand as he motioned me forward into his mother's kitchen. I could not wait to see if what Stacy said was true.

"Do you want to go to the prom?"

"Yeah, I want to go." He did not sound excited. "Look, Wendy, my mom said that she could afford only so much. I'm going to my dad's this weekend, and I'll ask him for some dough."

Lee made his way back to his bedroom, and I followed. He lay down on his side and closed his eyes. He reached out, motioning for me to sit down. I lay down in front of him, and he wrapped his left arm around me and pulled me close. Lee suffered from migraines. I knew if he was home from school, his head must have really been hurting.

"My mom said she would pay for the tickets," I whispered.

"I want to go. We'll work something out. Do not worry, babe." Lee's calming tone was reassuring.

We spooned in silence, and Lee drifted off to sleep. Before long, we heard the same quick two beeps outside.

Lee was awake. "Babe, that's Stacy." He gently kissed me on the nape of my neck and drew me closer against him as he tightened his arm around me.

"I do not want to go," I whispered.

"I know I do not want you to go. You got calc this period, right?"

"Yes, and I hate it," I whined.

"I know, but you can't miss it. Plus, Stacy came back for you. He's doing me a favor."

I slowly got up, and giving a few taps on my butt, Lee walked me to the kitchen door.

"Come on!" Stacy yelled out the car window. "We gotta make it before the second bell!"

"I'll call you tonight," Lee said. "I will work it out."

With a quick hug and kiss, I ran down the steps and slammed the car door.

"You good?" Stacy asked as he sped down Leahy Avenue back to school.

"Yes. Thank you, Stacy."

"No probs. Anything for my man. He's crazy about you, girl."

Stacy parked, we got out, and ran in a side door. The second bell rang as Ms. Worrell was coming to close her door. I slipped into my seat.

"Everyone please open your books to chapter 2. We will begin with derivatives."

I hated math.

That evening around six o'clock, the phone rang. My mother answered and called me over.

"Remember, don't stay on long in case he tries to call. Keep an eye out for the headlights of his car coming up the driveway."

She did not have to tell me. We both knew the ritual I had to follow every time I received calls from friends from school. Mommy allowed me to receive calls only if he was not home. If he was home, my friends knew to hang up. He did not allow calls or visits from friends, and I was not allowed to reciprocate.

Whenever Lee called, my heart smiled. He was the first and only boy that I was allowed to date. Technically, we had started dating in October, although we had been together long before that. Of course, for me, dates were not allowed, so we had to keep our relationship secret. For months, Lee asked when I would get up enough nerve to ask permission to date. He reminded me over and over that we had not officially gone out on a date. I told Lee how terrified I was to bring the subject up to him, but I knew that sooner or later, I had to muster up the courage. If I wanted to go to the prom, I could not pull some boy out of the air and say that he wanted to escort me. My father was too smart for that and would see right through the lie.

Lee was so courageous. One day, he said that he was tired of waiting and sneaking around, and he was going to call my father. Even after warning him that he probably would not be well received, and even if he were, he would be interrogated like a criminal, Lee remained dogmatic. I told Lee that I had to first find a time when it was safe to call. It was better after he had eaten his dinner and had a few vodkas. The plan was that I would sneak into my parent's bedroom and call Lee when I felt the coast was clear. Lee would then hang up and call back.

I waited for him to finish his dinner. After his first vodka, I snuck back to the master bathroom, closed the door, and walked through a door that led to my parent's bedroom to call Lee about my father's state of mind. "He seems to be in an okay mood. Give me five minutes to get back into the kitchen, and then call."

I walked back through the second door, flushed the toilet, and ran water from the faucet into the sink. I waited a minute and walked out of the bathroom, down the hallway, and into the kitchen. As I began to run water in the sink to wash the dinner dishes, pots, and pans, the phone rang. My body jumped from the piercing sound.

"Yello!" he quickly answered, as if knowing who was on the line. "This is he. Who is speaking? Oh, hiya doing, boy?"

I cringed at the accent.

"Yeah, I got time to talk. We are just finishing up dinner. What's on your mind?"

I swallowed deeply and slowly. My knees felt like they were going to fail me at any moment. The only thing that kept me up was knowing that Lee was being so brave for me. I held my breath and pretended not to sneak glances through the crisscrosses of the pass-through kitchen window opening over the sink. I focused on every word he said, trying to anticipate the next one.

"Well, my wife and I would like to sit down with your parents and discuss this," he said.

Discuss this? Oh, crap. I had not told him that Lee's father and mother were divorced. This was not good. He would frown upon the notion that Lee came from a single-parent household. No matter that divorce was normal and happened all the time, he still believed that any child coming from a single-parent home would be messed up for life. "Social misfits" he called them, another one of his ignorant and ironic misjudgments.

"My wife and I will be over. Looking forward to meeting your mother." He hung up the phone abruptly and called out, "Where is that boy's father?"

The question startled me so bad that it made me jump, sending dishwater splashing onto the floor. Before I could answer, his piercing, bloodshot eyes were pressed against the crisscross of the window grate openings from the other side in the family room.

"His mother and father are divorced," I said slowly.

"You didn't tell me that! Where's his pappy?"

"He remarried and lives in New York City."

"Ha! Ha!" He laughed loudly and said to my mother, who had come into the kitchen, "Wendy, we are going over to meet this boy's mammy on Saturday after supper. Did you know his parents were divorced?"

Mommy lied and said no. She dared not let on that she knew more than he did, because no one ever knew more than he. After I finished washing the dishes, I went to my room and attempted to complete my homework, but all I could think about was what Lee said over the phone.

Later, a soft knock came to the door. It was Mommy. She sat on the edge of my bed. "Well, at least he is going to meet Lee's mother," she whispered.

"I know. I hope he doesn't embarrass me any further. I hope he does not go over there talking in that fake Southern accent, and I hope he doesn't brag about how great he is and lie about being a Marine."

"Don't worry. It will be all right. Change into your night clothes, and get yourself ready for bed. Have you finished your homework?"

"No, I have a little calculus to do."

"Well, finish up, and then roll your hair and go to bed. Do you need my help with your homework?"

"No, I'm okay."

"Are you sure?"

"Yeah, Mom. I am okay."

"Okay. Do not worry. It will be all right. Have a good night, and Mommy loves you." She kissed my forehead and left the room, closing the door quietly behind her.

I never completed my homework, because my stomach was too upset with worry. Saturday was the day after tomorrow.

The next day, I could not get ready fast enough for school. I jumped out of bed before Mommy came to wake me. He had already gotten up and left for work. I quickly showered, brushed my teeth, and styled my hair. I thought about trying to complete the unfinished portion of my calculus homework, but it was only a few questions. I could compare notes with Susan Maloney in homeroom before going to class. Besides, my mind was focused on getting to school and talking to Lee. I carefully selected an outfit from my closet and dressed.

Mommy was already in the kitchen, preparing our lunches and breakfast. She always rose first, got herself ready, and then woke everyone else. She was scooping corned beef hash and scrambled eggs from the frying pan and carefully dividing them between two paper plates. By the time I poured some orange juice, she had retrieved the toast from the toaster and sat down to eat.

"Did you finish all your homework?"

"No, I still have a few problems to do for calculus."

"Well, go and get it, and I will help you."

"It's okay, Mom. I'm going to finish it in homeroom."

"Well, if you let me help you, you will have it done, and you will not be throwing anything down on paper."

"It's okay. They are easy. I can even do it in the car."

"I told you about doing your homework in the car. It will be sloppy."

"Okay, Mom."

I finished my last bit of hash and placed my plate in the trash. As I was gathering my books from my desk in my room, I heard the clicking of my mother's shoes. That meant she had washed the dishes, grabbed her school stuff and coat, and was heading out the door. I picked up the pink bottle from my dresser and spritzed a bit of Sweet Honesty behind both ears and on my neck.

For as long as I could remember, the rides from our house to Grandma and Granddaddy's or to school were filled with some type of emotion. They usually consisted of a debriefing of what occurred last night, what was to come that day, or both. On this morning, we debriefed about what occurred last night and what was to occur this weekend.

"Make sure you check with Lee today. Find out what time is good for us to come by tomorrow evening."

"Am I going?"

"No, just your father and me. Don't worry. It will be fine."

We stopped to pick up bagels and then pulled up outside the main gate of Sonderling High. I leaned over to give her my usual kiss on the cheek.

"Thanks, Mom. Love you. See you later."

CHAPTER 20

Meet the Parents

thought Saturday would never arrive. I rose feeling sick to my stomach with anticipation of how the day would unravel. Would he wake and decide at the last moment that they would not go over to Lee's house? Would he realize that I forgot to sweep the kitchen floor after dinner last night and use that against me as a reason not to go? Should I try to sneak down the hall and quickly sweep before he noticed? Maybe before he got up, I could put water on to boil for his coffee, and he would reward me for doing so. What if I started breakfast?

"Wendy!" His call rattled my thoughts. "I hope you are up and ready. We're going over to dat boy's house later on."

At the sound of his barking voice, I wanted to back out, but I was determined to see it through for better or worse. In the shower, I asked God to make everything all right today. Even if he beat me tomorrow, today had to be okay. I dressed quickly, combed my hair, grabbed my glasses, and followed the aroma of corned beef hash, sage sausage, and coffee to the kitchen.

After breakfast, Saturday's routine was pretty much the same. He went to school to oversee some athletic game going on, and Mommy and I did chores and shopping. The minutes went by like hours.

By five o'clock, Mommy was pulling the Monte Carlo into our L-shaped driveway. She said, "Let's hurry up and get these things in the house and put away so I can start dinner before he gets home. Don't forget to unload the dishwasher."

I put away the groceries while Mommy started dinner. We were having Hamburger Helper and broccoli. After I unloaded the dishwasher, I ran downstairs to get the towels and sheets out of the dryer. "Make sure nothing is damp and everything is dry," she yelled down to the basement. "Please fold the towels for Mommy, and put them away and make your bed up. When you are finished, get washed up and change your clothes. We told Lee's mother we would be there at eight, and I want you to eat before he gets here."

I quickly made my bed. I folded eight towels and put them away in the linen closet and made my way to the bathroom to wash up.

"Is your navy-blue skirt clean?" Mommy asked as she entered the bathroom from her bedroom door.

"Yes, it is, but…" I thought I was not coming with them. I also thought I would wear jeans.

"Okay, put that on with a white or beige blouse. Do you need stockings, or do you have a pair?"

"I have a pair."

"Make sure there are no runs in them, Wendy."

"There aren't, Mom."

"If your brown shoes need some polish, look in the drawer by the sink. There should be a small bottle of polish under there."

After I got dressed, I headed for the kitchen. I liked Hamburger Helper. It was like getting two meals in one: the hamburger and the cheesy macaroni. As I was making my plate, Mommy entered wearing her fluffy pink bathrobe.

"Mom, do you want me to fix your plate?"

"No, baby, I will eat when he gets here, which should be shortly."

I glanced up at the clock, which read six thirty. "He is going to be late, isn't he?" I asked with a tremor of fear in my voice. "Wendy, he knows we need to be there at eight o'clock." I sat down to eat, but my nerves were getting the best of me, and I was not able to enjoy one of my favorite meals. The sound of a car door slam made me jump in my seat.

Our eyes met. "Hurry up and finish—"

"Wendy!" he called out, slamming the front door behind him. "Where ya at, girl? You know we meetin' that boy and his mammie at eight o'clock. Is my dinner ready?" He entered the kitchen. "How's my baby girl?"

"Good," I said, relieved that he sounded as though he was in a good mood—for now, anyway.

"Hey girl!" he said to Mommy as he slapped her on the ass. "We ready to eat?"

"Yes, Robert, your tray is all set up."

"Well, did you eat?"

"No, I was waiting for you to get home."

"Okay, well then, get a move on. I need to take a shower." He went into the family room and sat in his chair where his TV tray was set up with his plate piled high. A slice of white bread lay on a napkin next to a tall glass of Coca-Cola with ice. "I'm gonna say grace. You too slow."

He shoveled the food in his mouth and then went to the bathroom to shower. I made quick work of clearing the plates and washed the dishes. Minutes later, we all jumped in the car.

"Where does this boy live?" he asked as he backed out of the driveway. It was 7:25, and we had less than forty minutes to arrive.

"He lives on Leahy Avenue," I said with a bit of authority.

"Well, what is the address, pumpkin? Do you think I am a psychic?"

"Sixteen, the address is 16 Leahy Avenue."

"Isn't that across the tracks?"

"I think so," I lied. I knew exactly where it was. I had been there many times. It was across the tracks, blocks away from the tenth grade center. What did it matter that it was across the tracks? He seemed to forget that when we relocated to Long Island, we had lived "across the tracks" in another town for some time before we moved. He was so judgmental.

"What is his mama's name again?"

"Her name is Melba, Melba Clarke."

"And what is his pappy's name?"

"He was named after his father, and his father's name is Lee Clarke."

"Is his father going to be there?" He sped down Bay Shore Road.

"No, Lee lives with his mother, and his father lives in the city. Brooklyn, to be exact." All these facts had been given to him last week and as early as yesterday. I knew he wanted to relish in what he considered a lower economic level. I hated it when he operated that way. It was so disgusting. He obviously forgot where he came from.

"Oh, yeah. His mammie and pappy are divorced," he said as if he just had a revelation. "Well, she must have gotten the short end of the stick to be living over in that hell hole. Wendy, we need to make sure we get out of there before it gets too dark. I do not want any problems with parking my car in that neighborhood for too long. I should have brought my pistol. When I point to my watch, we start getting out of there, understand?" He looked at Mommy in a threatening way as if she did not have a choice.

"Yes, Robert."

"We ain't eating none of their food or drinking nothing. We're just coming so they can see what kind of people we are and decide about this prom."

Finally, we arrived on Leahy Avenue. The road was dimly lit. One of the streetlights must have gone out. I hoped that he did not notice, as that would be all he would need to back out.

"Damn, you can hardly see down this mutha. What's the number again, Wendy?"

"Sixteen, 16 Leahy," I answered nervously.

"Damn. Let me turn around in the schoolyard and put my high beams on and go down this street again." We pulled into the tenth grade center, and he turned the Monte Carlo around. We emerged again on the street, this time with high beams on and driving slowly. "Damn. I can't see shit!"

I knew exactly where the house was in the light or dark because I had cut class so many times to go there with Lee. I saw the light on in the kitchen when we drove down the street the first time. I needed a moment to gather my nerves and calm myself down, so I allowed him to pass by their house, but I needed to speak up, or I could risk him leaving altogether.

"There, there it is. It is the one with the blue van in the driveway and the black car behind it."

"Whose van is that?" he asked in a disgusting manner.

"His mother's, and the black car is his," I said in a proud manner.

"Damn, she really did get the short end of the stick. That van is older than me. The boy's car looks like it is in a little better shape. You didn't tell me that boy had a car, Wendy." His voice was growing louder. "You haven't been in that car, have you?"

"No, I haven't," I lied.

"I better not see you in that car. They probably do not have any insurance."

I hated his pompous attitude.

"Well, I guess I will pull up here." As he pulled the car alongside the road in front of Lee's house, my nerves were getting the best of me. "Well, come on. What are you waiting for?" He waved his hands, motioning for me to get out of the car. I pushed the seat forward and crawled out. The silent night made the clicking of our heels sound like a synchronized tap dance. The small, white porch light lit the side of the house, but the front door was dark. They never used the front entrance, because it was sealed off. Everyone entered on the side through the kitchen. I never asked why.

"Why don't they have the light on in the front?" he whispered to Mommy.

"I don't know, Robert. Let's go over to the side where the light is on."

"I see the damn light," he said in a louder, defiant tone. Now he was standing in the middle of the dark driveway. I was hoping they were not peering out, looking at us. I was so embarrassed. Finally, he rang the doorbell.

Ms. Melba Clarke was a free-spirited, friendly, Christian woman. "Hello!" she sang out, almost as if she were performing in a choir. She arrived at the screen door.

"Ms. Clarke." Miraculously, he lost the fake country accent and replaced it with the King's English. "My name is Robert Howell, and I am here with my wife and my daughter." I guess he forgot our names.

"C'mon in," she sang as she opened the door and waved us in. The aroma of fried chicken filled the room. "Would you have some chicken, Wendy? There is plenty left."

I felt the heat of his eyes piercing the left side of my face. Before I could answer, Mommy jumped in to save me. "No, no thanks. We have already eaten."

"Well, maybe a little later." Lee's mother sounded hopeful. "Lee! Wendy is here with her parents." She said to us, "He got home from football practice not long ago. I know he is tired. Let us have a seat."

Lee emerged from his bedroom. He was so fine. His athletic build was perfect for a star quarterback. His shoulders were not too broad but still seemed strong enough to carry the weight of the world. I loved running my fingers through his hair—it was so soft and wavy. It seemed like he always wore a smile. He was wearing his rectangle gold-framed glasses. He must have been studying, and his glasses made him look mysteriously sexy. I had never realized it before, but I think he was the same height as me or slightly taller. I stood five foot five, and he must have been five foot seven. He had a slow deliberate stride to his walk.

Since I was facing the door, I saw him first as he came out, and he looked at me with a confidant, calming smile. His smile melted me every time. "Hey kiddo," he said as he lightly touched my shoulder.

I responded in a soft tone. "Hey."

He put his hand out toward Mommy. "Hi there, Mrs. Howell. Nice to meet you."

Whew! He was too cool and calm for me. He spoke on the phone with Mommy more than with me. Whenever he called and she answered the phone, she always pretended it was the wrong number. That was the signal that he was home and I was not allowed to come to the phone. When he was fast asleep on the couch in the family room, Mommy would make her way quietly down the hall to tell me, "Lee called. Hurry up and use the phone in my room, and I will go back and keep a watch over him. Do not talk long. He may wake up." Mommy managed to bring some sort of normalcy to our lives even though the environment dictated otherwise.

"Nice to meet you as well, Lee," Mommy said with a slight, unassuming smile.

He rose to his feet and extended his hand. "My name is Robert, Robert Howell. I am Wendy's father."

No kidding, I thought. *Who else would he be? Our gardener?*

He spoke with such force that you would have thought he was responding to a military command. He grabbed Lee's hand, drew him near, and shook it as if he was trying to yank it off. Another one of his intimidation tactics.

Lee rolled with the punches. He knew who and what he was dealing with, and he kept that warm, inviting smile plastered across his face. After my father released Lee's hand, Lee took a seat next to his mother on the sofa facing us. Throughout the conversation, we snuck looks at each other. When our eyes met, we looked away. Lee knew about my nerves, and his frequent glances in my direction were to reassure and comfort me. It was working.

"Looka here, these kids got this prom coming up, and we want to know what you plan on doing."

I was so embarrassed by his dictatorship-like tone. I snuck a glance at Lee, who continued to smile.

"Well, Lee would love to accompany Wendy to her prom, and we are prepared to pay for her corsage, Lee's lapel flower, and the tuxedo rental. Lee can drive his car." Ms. Melba's sweet, kind tone was consistent with her personality.

His rude, abrupt demeanor quickly swallowed it up. "My girl will have the best, so we're getting a limousine for her and your boy." He scanned the room as if looking for a missing object. "Sooooo, Wendy tells me your husband left ya."

I was mortified. I wanted to sink into the couch. Mommy twisted on the couch. I snuck a look across at Lee, and his smile turned into a long stare.

"Lee's father and I are divorced." Her tone remained polite.

"Well, seeing he is not here and all, we will pick up the cost for all the pictures, as many as my girl wants. There will be few in there for you too." He was relentless in his obnoxious, rude behavior. "Wendy, are we buying the tickets too?" Before Mommy could respond, he continued to spew venom. "Yeah, we paying for that too. Heh, heh, we almost paying for the whole damn thing, ain't we?"

He gave Mommy two quick slaps on her knee. Mommy could barely maintain her nervous smile, and Lee was clenching his jaw. I wanted to run out of there.

He looked at his watch, the signal that it was time to go. "Well, that settles it. We need to get on down the road." He rose off the couch with a proud peacock stance and walked over to Lee to shake his hand. "Nice meeting ya, young man. I got my eye on you."

Lee jumped off the couch so quickly that I thought he would sucker punch my father. "Good to meet you too, sir. You were all that Wendy says you were." Lee's slightly sarcastic grin let me know that he was throwing a subtle jab.

Lee's mother stood and motioned my father toward the kitchen and the side door. Mommy stood up in front of me and glanced back at Lee with a smile. I was the last to follow.

I whispered to Lee, "I am so sorry."

He grabbed my right hand and quickly met my right ear with his soft lips. "It's okay. He is an asshole. I love you, kid." He kissed my ear. I held his hand as long as I could and gave it a quick squeeze as I headed out the side door.

He was yelling at me from the car. "C'mon, Wendy, we gotta get out of this place. It's getting dark." I turned back to look at Lee and mouthed, "I love you too."

He gave me a wink and waved.

CHAPTER 21

The Dress

The Sonderling High prom was the event of the year. This was an opportunity to give seniors a chance to enjoy an evening of fun, food, and friends while creating lifelong memories.

Preparing for the prom was a mini event in and of itself. All the girls were getting their prom dresses from South Shore Mall. Mommy said that for such a special day, "you don't want to see yourself coming and going." She said she would take me into New York City to find a dress from a boutique bridal store. My father was not keen on the idea, especially since his idea of New York City was a place filled with welfare recipients in low-income housing projects, drugs, and crime. It was not a place for women to be walking around, yet his Masonic lodge, the place he frequented for those weekend lodge meetings, was located there. I do not know how she convinced him.

A month before prom, I was clearing his dinner plate one night when he said, "So your mother tells me you and she are going dress shopping into the city tomorrow. I don't want no daughter of mine having some regular dress, so you make sure you find something great. I gave your momma the checkbook, so do not worry about price. You find a real pretty dress, you hear me?"

"Yes, sir."

I knew about boutique bridal stores in New York from the ads in women's magazines. They had some of the most beautiful bridal gowns, and women around the world shopped there. Seniors were given permission to have Thursday off to prepare for the prom and only came in on Friday to pick up the invitations, yearbooks, and cap and gowns and hand in any last-minute assignments since prom was early that evening. Thursday morning, we rode in silence as Mommy drove to First Avenue between Fourth Street and Brentwood Road to the Brentwood train station. I was thinking about what New York City was really like, because I did not believe the things my father said. I wondered if all the dresses would look as magnificent in person as they did in the magazines. I wondered what deal Mommy had to make with him to bring me to this place.

Ten minutes into the train ride, I broke my silence. "Mom, is he really letting us go into the city today? Is he going to be there?" It seemed too good to be true.

"Yes, baby, we are going to the city, but he will not be there."

"How do you know?"

"I know because he has school, and games after school, so he will be in Westbury all day."

I was relieved and allowed myself to settle in and enjoy the ride. Station after station, the closer we got to the city, more riders boarded. We arrived at Penn Station an hour later.

"Wendy, stay close to me, and pay attention."

I had never been among so many people at one time. Everyone seemed to be in a rush and going different directions. The hustle and bustle of the streets filled me with energy and excitement.

"Wendy, we need to make our way to the street so we can catch a cab."

The busyness of Penn Station mirrored the street level activity. The never-ending sea of yellow cabs, coupled with thick exhaust smells, blanketed the streets as far as the eye could see. So many cars were bumper to bumper, honking their monotone horns. The aroma of hot dogs and pizza ushered me into the experience. As we walked down the street, the odor of wet garbage from the steam rising from the manholes briefly usurped the hot dog and pizza aroma. I felt as though I was in a bumper car ride at the carnival as I bumped off one person after another. My eyes followed the scaffolding and buildings that scaled high to the sky.

We found a spot on the pavement, and Mommy raised her hand like a pro to hail a cab. The smell of fresh-baked onion bagels enveloped us—it was mesmerizing and intoxicating. I inhaled deeply, wanting to take the smell with me.

A cab stopped, and we jumped in. The smell of sweat and fast food ripped me out of the euphoric onion bagel aroma. I masked my nose and mouth with my jean jacket collar. If I could have pulled it over my head to protect me from the stench, I would have, but I knew Mommy would not allow that behavior in public. I don't know how she withstood it without covering her nose and mouth. I wanted to pass out as my eyes watered. Thank goodness the ride to the bridal boutique was short.

On this morning, the boutique was humming with excitement. Small groups of women were waiting patiently while others were chatting among themselves. A woman of average height, dressed in all black, walked over to greet us with a polite smile. "Welcome ladies. Do you have an appointment with us today?"

"Yes, my daughter and I have a ten o'clock appointment," Mommy said.

"Okay, great. Follow me. I will get you checked in, and then a bridal consultant will be out to greet you."

We waited about fifteen minutes in the waiting area, and a smiling consultant came out to greet us. "Hello, Mrs. Howell. My name is Louise, and I am your bridal consultant today."

As Mommy introduced us, my investigative eyes were distracted. I scanned the showroom of elegantly dressed mannequins and sparkly bridal accessories. We were escorted to a private dressing room. The consultant began interviewing us to determine selections.

"Well, she is only seventeen, so a modest, off-the shoulder tea length with a fitted waist could be an option."

"It has to be ice blue." I chimed in because the limo was midnight blue.

"Okay. Well, now that I have an idea, I will be back with some selections."

A few moments passed, and Louise arrived with six dresses. Only two were light blue, and the others were a sand color. The first was an A-line with a silk bodice. It was okay but not the one. The second dress I tried on was a sand-colored, ankle-length silk gown with spaghetti straps and a scooped neckline. Not the one.

After the fifth dress, I excused myself to go to the ladies' room. As I made my way back to the dressing room, I froze. Stunning, elegant, and elaborate—it was the gown that I knew I could not leave without. The brilliant white gown had a delicately designed, gold lace mesh overlay with tiny, gold flowers intricately placed throughout. It took my breath away. The sleeves were delicately puffed but not pronounced. The exaggerated V-neck was slightly lower than anything I owned but still elegant. The delicately cinched waist was complimented by a dainty, white rosebud piped in gold. The train was overstated in length with the continuation of the gold flowers throughout the gold lace mesh overlay. It was a showstopper.

When I returned to the dressing room, the consultant had replaced the previous selections with other options, but I never gave them a second look. I spoke rapidly, "Mommy, I saw the gown that I want. It's the most beautiful thing in the world, it's white and gold, and it's on the mannequin in the middle of the store, can I try it on, please, please?"

"Well, Wendy, take a breath. The nice woman has brought in some other options. Don't you want to at least see what they look like on?"

"Mom, I can try them on, but I know I won't like them. Will you come and see the dress? I know you will love it like I do."

"Okay. We can ask the nice woman to see if she can bring in the one you saw. Let's go take a look at it first."

When she saw it, Mommy looked as if she had hit the lottery. She stood still and just stared at it with a smile. She was at a loss for words. I turned around, and there it was.

"Wendy, one of the girls told me you were admiring this stunner. Would you like to try it on?" Louise said.

I looked at Mommy for approval, and her mouth was still hanging open. "Mom, can I?"

"Yes, of course," she whispered.

"Now I want you to know, Mrs. Howell, that your daughter has selected a wedding dress from our premiere collection. She has exquisite taste. This masterpiece has a few ways it can be worn. We will try without the hoop, but we showcase it with the hoop for more of an overstated effect."

Louise placed a pair of white, three-inch pumps in the middle of the platform. She placed the unzipped dress carefully over the shoes. "Wendy, I would like you to slowly step into the shoes and I will support you.

I stepped into the shoes, and Louise slowly pulled the gown up and zipped me up. She turned me around in the mirror. The words would not come. I glanced at Mommy's reflection, and she had tears in her eyes.

"She looks like a princess, Mrs. Howell."

Without the hoop, the dress was beautiful, but with it, it was breathtaking. Mommy whispered, "We will have Mrs. James give you an updo with soft baby curls coming down."

"Mrs. Howell, we have a slight problem. This is a wedding dress with an attached train."

Louise, I do not want her to have the train, because it is not her wedding day. Can you have it removed without taking away from the look of the dress?"

Louise placed her left index finger to her closed lips. "Hmmm, that is an idea. Allow me to consult with our seamstress to see if and how that would be done."

"Mommy, I really want this dress."

Before Mommy could respond, Louise returned and said, "Well, today is your lucky day. I have spoken with the seamstress, and she can remove the train with little to no effort."

I glanced over at Mommy for approval.

"Thank you, Louise. What would be the time frame for this work to be completed?"

Louise returned her finger to her lips. "Well, the good thing is that you are one of the first appointments of the day. If you can busy yourself in the city for a few hours, I am sure she can have it ready for you to take with you today."

"Yes!" I exclaimed.

"That would be fine. We will get something to eat and return in an hour or so. Would that be fine?"

"Yes, that will be perfect. Wendy, let's get you out of this dress so we can get started as soon as possible."

I leaned on Mommy's right shoulder as I stepped out of the gown. Louise cupped her left arm around my waist and carefully pulled the dress down and away from the podium.

On our way out, we walked around for a few blocks and came upon a bagel shop where we were able to indulge in toasted onion bagels with cream cheese and orange juice. We then came upon a small restaurant where we were able to get breakfast. After an hour, we made our way back.

Louise was waiting for us. "Your timing is perfect. The seamstress is steaming the dress now, and I know you and Wendy will be pleased. It should not be much longer."

Mommy and I busied ourselves, flipping through bridal magazines. Before long, Louise returned with the dress on a hanger and another woman carrying an off-white garment bag. "Please take a look," Louise said cheerfully. "She did a masterful job."

With the skillful eye of a teacher, Mommy examined the back and then the front. She turned to me. "Wendy, what do you think?"

I brushed my hand across the soft gold lace. "Mommy, thank you so much. I love it."

Louise motioned to the woman holding the garment bag, and they carefully placed the dress inside. She handed it to me. "Careful to hold it up high, or you can gently fold it across your arm when travelling." Louise bade us a goodbye.

Mommy hailed a cab, and we were soon back at Penn Station, waiting for the train to Brentwood. "As soon as we get home, hang the gown up so it will not get wrinkled. You may have to push some of the clothes back farther in your closet to make room." Mommy closed her eyes and tilted her head toward the window. All I could think about was what Lee would say when he saw me in this beautiful gown. I was sure I would not see myself coming and going at the prom.

As the train pulled into the Brentwood station, Mommy already had her car keys in her hand.

"Wendy, come on, hurry up so I can get home and get dinner started, and you can hang the gown up so it will not get wrinkled. I have papers to grade and need to turn in my grades tomorrow."

"Mom, I can help grade papers or log the grades in your gradebook." I loved helping Mommy grade papers or write the grades in her green spiral-bound gradebook.

"Wendy, have you completed all of your assignments and turned them in?"

"Yes, Mommy, I finished my English essay already. I just need to turn it in."

"Do you have any library books that need to be brought back?'

"I just have to put them in my bookbag."

"Well, make sure you do that first."

We pulled into the driveway, and as I was on my way into the house, Mommy called after me.

"When you are done in your room, bring your essay so I can read it over while the food is cooking."

Kindergarten to twelfth grade, our homework was checked for neatness and correctness before we turned it in to be graded. Mommy always tried to make sure she looked at it first so that by the time he got home, there would be no need. However, sometimes, if he was home early, he would make us sit at the kitchen table and stand over us, grilling us on what we had to do whether it was math, science, social studies, or English. He always knew more than the teachers and ridiculed their teaching styles and homework assignments. There were a few times he did not agree with a grade we received after he offered what he thought was the right answer and challenged the teacher. One time, he asked my social studies teacher to call him to explain why I earned a B on a paper that he helped me with and forced the teacher to change the grade to an A or he was going to come up to the school and have a word with him. I was so embarrassed.

"Wendy, hurry up so we can be on time!"

We hurried down the station steps and made our way to the car. My stomach was a ball of nerves. We were on our way to Georgette James's house in Wyandanch. Mrs. James had a beauty parlor in the basement, and Mommy and I had appointments every two weeks on Friday to get our hair done. At some appointments, only I got my hair done, and Mommy washed hers on the weekend. This was one of those times—yet another sacrifice that Mommy made when money was low.

Mrs. James was sitting at the shampoo bowl reading *Ebony* when we arrived.

"Well, good afternoon. I hear today is a special day for someone."

"Good afternoon, Mrs. James. Yes, today is my prom."

"I remember my prom. Do you remember yours, Mrs. Howell?"

"Yes, I do." Mommy smiled as if remembering good times.

"Well, what are we getting done today?"

I looked at Mommy for direction.

"Well, Mrs. James, we would like a soft updo with small curls at the top."

"What color is your dress, Wendy?"

"It is white with a beautiful gold lace overlay with slightly puffed sleeves. The waist has a small, white rose piped in gold on the left side. Oh, and it has a hoop underneath so the dress spreads out."

"Oh, my. It sounds absolutely beautiful like a princess dress. Well, we will get you more beautiful than you are and ready for that prom. You will be the talk of the town." Mrs. James created the exact look that Mommy was looking for. She turned me around in the chair and reached for the mirror.

"I love it, Mrs. James. Thank you."

"Mrs. Howell, do you approve?"

Mommy had the same beautiful smile as when she first saw me in the dress. "Mrs. James, it is perfect. Would you mind spraying it a bit for hold?"

"Oh, certainly. That goes without saying." Mrs. James grabbed the can of Aqua Net and lightly sprayed my head.

"Wendy, you make sure you take a lot of pictures and have a great time."

"Thank you, Mrs. James."

Mommy paid, and we were on our way. She said, "Wendy, we are going to make a quick stop by Mrs. Spencer's. She wants to see you before the prom, and then we have to go to the market for a few things."

"Okay, Mommy."

As we entered Grandma Spencer's kitchen, the faint aroma of sage sausage collided with the aroma of hamburgers.

"Wendy, Mrs. James did a wonderful job on your hair," Grandma said.

"Thank you, Grandma."

"Well, I wasn't sure what time your mom was coming by today, so I have leftover sage sausage from breakfast. I can scramble some eggs and add some cheese. I was fixing a little lunch for Grandaddy, and there are chips on the table. Mrs. Howell, I am sure you can stay for a little something to eat."

I looked at Mommy for approval before sitting down at the table that was set with Grandma's day china.

"I guess we can stay a little while. We were on our way to Pathmark to pick up a few things and are not due back to the house for a while."

"Wonderful! Well, have a sit down. Wendy, what would you like?"

"May I have a cheeseburger, please?" I loved Grandma's cheeseburgers. She cooked them with fresh red onions inside. When you bit into the burger, the mild sweetness of the onion paired well with the juicy burger that rested on crisp lettuce and the sharp flavor of the melted cheese. She always toasted the bun, giving it a slight crust on the outside and a soft middle. The sliver of mayo and ketchup ratio was just enough and didn't overwhelm the fresh ingredients from Granddaddy's garden. I couldn't wait and sat at the table, awaiting the experience.

"Yes, you may," Grandma said. "If there are not enough chips in the bag, I have another one in the cabinet. You know Grandaddy loves chips, so I am not sure what he left behind."

"Mrs. Spencer, there are enough. We are fine."

Grandma sat a glass pitcher of freshly brewed sweet tea with lemon slices in the middle of the table and removed the bag of half-eaten Lays potato chips. She returned with a plate of cheeseburgers, a new bag of Lays, and a jar of Vlasic sliced pickles.

"There is plenty, so help yourselves."

While I went in for a cheeseburger, Grandma opened the bag of Lays, spread a generous amount on our plates, and poured tea for all. I placed two slices of pickles on my bun and a few chips on top and prepared my mouth for a big bite. The chorus of flavors blended, creating a party in my mouth. To this day, I relish in a delicious, juicy cheeseburger with all the accoutrements.

"Wendy, Mrs. Spencer is speaking to you!" Mommy's firm voice snapped me out of my bliss.

"It's okay, Mrs. Howell. She is not being disrespectful. She is enjoying her cheeseburger."

Grandma was right. I was enjoying my food so much that I didn't realize she was speaking to me.

"Are you excited about your prom? What color dress did you decide?"

"Yes, I am, Grandma. I can't wait. We went to a boutique in Manhattan, and I found the most beautiful dress. It is white with a gold lace overlay."

"Wow. Boutique? Only the best for the best. Well, you better make sure you take a lot of pictures."

"Mrs. Spencer, we will. We paid for professional pictures and will make sure you get one."

We finished our burgers, and I helped Grandma clear the plates. "Mrs. Spencer, that was delicious, and we thank you."

"Mrs. Howell, I am so tickled you and Wendy stopped by so that I could see her hair and we could all have a bite to eat. I will be right back. I want to give Wendy something."

"Oh, Mrs. Spencer, you don't have to—"

Before Mommy could finish her sentence, Grandma was out the door. "Wendy, go to the bathroom if you need to, and get yourself ready so when Mrs. Spencer returns, we can go."

When I came out of the bathroom, Grandma and Mommy were arranging flowers on the table. Mommy pulled out the dining room chair. "Wendy, have a seat."

Grandma had selected some sprigs of white baby's breath and gently placed a few in my hair. "Mrs. Howell, what do you think?"

"Mrs. Spencer, they make the perfect finishing touch."

I went to the bathroom to look in the mirror. The baby's breath gave my hair a regal finishing touch. I loved it.

"Wendy, I am going to send you home with some extra baby's breath in case you need to freshen up these later."

"Thank you, Grandma."

We left for Pathmark. Mommy picked up a few groceries, and we made our way home so that I could get ready for the prom.

I called Lee to check in. He said that he was finishing cutting the grass and was on his way to pick up my wristlet. When he returned, he would start getting ready. I reminded him that the limo would pick him up first, and he assured me he would be on time.

"Wendy, dinner is served. I think you should eat something so you have something on your stomach."

My stomach was a ball of nerves, but I managed to eat a chicken leg and a few forkfuls of mashed potatoes. On the way home, Mommy had stopped at Kentucky Fried Chicken to get a bucket of chicken, mashed potatoes and gravy, and string beans. She said she had no intention of cooking, because she wanted to help me get ready.

The front door slamming made me jump as I washed the dishes.

He marched his way into the kitchen. "How is my baby girl? You 'bout ready for tonight? What time is that boy getting here?" As he peered through the pass-through window between the family room and kitchen, his bloodshot eyes and the vodka vapors from his breath told me all I needed to know. I hoped he did not mess this up for me. I was full of anxiety and excitement and couldn't wait to see Lee.

"Momma, wash up the rest of those dishes. My baby got a prom to go to! Where is your mother?"

Mommy was coming up from the basement with a load of clothes. "I am here, Robert, and I will fix your plate in one minute."

"Well, I ain't hungry yet. I'll eat after that boy gets here. You can pass me a glass with some ice cubes." Another drink was something he did not need.

Mommy had my undergarments laid out on my bed. The hoop was hanging on the back of my door, and my dress was hanging in my closet. My white pumps were at the foot of the bed. My bag with the tickets inside was on my pillow, and Mommy's white pearl-drop earrings were next to it. When I came out of the shower, Mommy was waiting for me. She checked my hair to make sure it did not need touching up.

"Baby, sit down so I can put the fresh baby's breath in your hair. Then I will give it a light spray." Mommy applied a dusting of Fashion Fair powder on my face to keep the shine down and put the compact in my bag. I put on my undergarments while she removed the hoop from the hanger.

"Lean on me, and carefully step into this." The A-line crinoline wires were light and flexible, and once Mommy tied it in the back, it forced me into a perfect elegant posture. She pulled my desk chair to the middle of the floor. "I want to see how you sit down and stand up a few times." The first few times were a little awkward, but I quickly got the hang of it. She pulled the dress over my head and slowly zipped me up. She stepped back to look, and her eyes welled with joy. "You look stunning. I want to take a few pictures, and then you can walk out and let your father see you."

"Wendy, get a move on. That boy should be here soon!" he yelled.

"Slip your shoes on. I will see you in a minute," Mommy said.

As I slowly made my way down the hallway, camera flashes blinded me. Once they stopped, there my father stood with his hands in his pockets, grinning from ear to ear. As I walked closer, he wiped a tear from his bloodshot eye and hugged me. He lightly kissed me on my cheek, slowly circled me, and stopped in front of me. "Baby, you look beautiful."

The beep of a horn broke the moment. "Let me get my shoes on. That boy is here." He returned to the living room.

"Come, let's get the rest of your things." Mommy rushed to her bedroom. I grabbed my bag and took one last look in the white framed, full-length mirror.

Mommy came in and grabbed my bag out of my hand. "Let me have your bag. I am putting in two twenties and a ten in case you need it for any incidentals."

"Mommy, I don't—"

Before I could say I did not need the money, she left. I told myself I would not spend it so that I could return most of it to her. Lee said the plan was to meet a group at Friendly's after the prom. He worked a few days after school and on the weekend, so he always paid for our dates, but my mother and father always gave me money just in case.

Lee made his way inside the house and was making small talk with my father in the foyer.

As I approached Lee, he was beaming. His smile was wide, and his eyes lit up with joy. I was used to this look, because that was the way he always greeted me: as if it were the first time. I loved it. I loved him.

"Wow, you look beautiful, kid."

"Thank you, Lee. You look great."

"Yeah, I think she looks beautiful too, 'cause she's my daughter."

I ignored my father's passive-aggressive tone.

"I have your wristlet. Can I put it on?"

"Yeah, put it on her. She can't do it herself."

Mommy invited my father into the kitchen.

With the precision of a surgeon, Lee slid the corsage onto my left wrist. It was adorned with four small, white carnations, a yellow rose, and sprinklings of baby's breath. My floral-laced, white-gloved hands provided a backdrop of sophistication and femininity. My father returned and handed me Lee's boutonniere. I used a pearl-tipped hat pin and, with precision and a slight pressure, pierced the wrapped stem and gently secured Lee's white boutonniere to his lapel. He was stunningly handsome in his white tuxedo, canary-yellow cummerbund with matching bow tie, and white dress shoes.

Mommy took many more pictures before we were out the door and headed to the shiny, black limousine. My father pulled Lee back and spoke into his ear before he let him go. As I got into the limousine, Lee was right behind me, helping me pick up the dress so it did not drag on the ground.

"What did he say to you?" I asked.

He put his arm around me and drew me closer.

"You smell good."

"Who loves you?" he said.

"You do," I whispered.

"That's all you need to know." He flashed that warm smile that always made me feel so safe.

We arrived at the venue, and everyone looked great in their suits and gowns. We sat at a table with four other couples. The tables were beautifully set, and the food was okay. We did not eat much because we were so busy talking, walking around to visit friends at their tables, posing for pictures, and dancing. While we danced to a slow song, Lee held me close and whispered in my ear, "You look so beautiful, kiddo." His warm smile revealed his perfectly white teeth and melted my heart every time. My eyes closed as I rested my head on his shoulder. We held hands and slow dragged to "You Give Good Love." I wanted this moment to last forever.

Before the prom ended, a group of us decided to go to Friendly's and grab some food and dessert. We ate cheeseburgers and sundaes and talked until closing time. Lee and I said our goodbyes and headed out.

Lee asked the driver to take us to a place where we could have some quiet time alone and chill before he had to take me home. Within minutes, we pulled up to a parking area where it looked like other people had the same idea, as other limousines with fogged-up windows were parked there.

The driver said he would be back in an hour. He lit a cigarette and walked into the night toward a nearby diner.

CHAPTER 22

NCCU

t was time to go away to college. Instead of being elated to get out from under my father, I was terrified for my mother.

As she was so famous for doing, Mommy tried to maintain a positive spin on everything. "Wendy, you only have a couple months to go. We need to start getting your things put aside so you will know what you are packing. Mom Mom sent you a package the other day at school. We need to go by on Saturday when he is at practice and pick it up."

"Okay, Mom," I said even though I still had not agreed to the college plan. We had our own plan, our pact: when my brother and I finished high school, my brother, mother, and I would all flee. We never knew where—somewhere far away, just as long as we were together. Leaving Mommy with him was not an option. It was not part of the plan.

I did not have a choice. He wanted me to attend an all-black college. Knowing what I know now, I would not be so quick to refer someone to an all-black college. Coming from our neighborhood in Long Island, I was used to being called disparaging names by white people. That was a given. However, I was not equipped to be discriminated against by my own. The year I spent in Durham at North Carolina Central University (NCCU), I experienced interracial discrimination of the highest form. I thought I would meet people from different parts of the country and build great relationships. This was not to be.

I wanted to pledge a sorority but was told my skin was not light enough and my hair was not long enough. I was told I would be a better fit for the Deltas or Zetas. The fact that I was from the North did not bode well either. Anyone from New York, Philadelphia, Connecticut, New Jersey, and some parts of Delaware did not mingle well with students from south of the Mason-Dixon Line. Many of them had ignorant misconceptions about people from up North. We were referred to as Yankees, drug dealers, thieves, and other derogatory names. Fights in the male and female dorms—North versus South—were not uncommon: light skinned versus dark skinned, fraternities versus fraternities, and sororities versus sororities. I was called *darkie, ugly, buckwheat,* and other disparaging names. If it was not my skin, I was referred to as *honkie lover* because I spoke the King's English.

I had to say that students from the North gave it to the students from the South as well. They were called *country time, hillbillies, country asses, Uncle Toms, trailer park, slaves,* and other terms. The funny thing was that as much as the people from the South hated on the people from the North, they copied our fashion, hairstyles, music, dance moves, and anything else that was on trend.

My roommate, Rochelle, was from High Point, North Carolina, and we got along well. We were both freshmen raised in upper middle-class families, and our parents vowed that since we were freshman, they did not want us to be alone on campus over weekends or holidays if at all possible. My mother came to visit every other weekend. She rented a car and stayed at a hotel close to campus. She took Rochelle and me to the grocery store to stock up on groceries and then to the mall to shop. Whatever she purchased for me, she purchased for Rochelle, as she did not believe in doing for one and not the other. At night, Mommy ordered pizza for the floor, and the girls would go in and out of our dorm room, eating slices and hanging around to gossip. These were some of the better times at college. On the last night before she left, she took Rochelle and me out to dinner and made sure that we had leftovers to take back to the room in case we wanted a snack later that night or the next day.

Goodbyes were long because I hated to see her go. "Mommy will be back in a couple of weeks," she always said. I hated to think about her being alone with him until then.

On alternate weekends, I went to Rochelle's home in High Point.

Being away at college was both good and bad. The good was being out of the clutches of my father, being able to breathe, think, and navigate through life without living in constant fear, looking over my shoulder, on pins and needles, unsure of the next attack. The tormenting part was being away from home, leaving Mommy to endure the abuse alone, without Robert or me to absorb some of the blows.

CHAPTER 23

Found

The screeching of tires woke her from semiconsciousness. She was too afraid to look.

She scrunched down as far as she could as a car door slammed behind her and footsteps approached. She was in the parking lot off the New Jersey Turnpike, Exit 8. My mother crouched in her car as footsteps approached.

Is it him?

Will he get me?

Will this be the end?

Another car had screeched to a stop behind her car. Another car door slammed.

"Sis, it's me, Mike! Joe, come over here. She's here! We found her!"

CHAPTER 24

The Whys, You Ask

Forgive him!
Forgive him!
You must forgive him!
Those words are like fingernails scratching down a chalkboard. I feel fire in my eyes, burning higher and hotter the more the words are repeated, my brown pupils replaced with amber-red flame.

When people ask me about him, don't they expect that my response will be foul, especially when they ask about anything that occurred pre-adulthood?

Perhaps I am expecting *Girl, I know exactly what you mean* or *wow, I cannot believe a person is capable of doing such horrific things.* That at least makes it sound like they understand or sympathize. It would suffice. Better than the folks who respond with the infamous *I sympathize with what you are saying.* I have grown so tired of hearing this that I cannot distinguish sincere sympathy from robotic words.

It would be nice to hear *Girl, what you and your family went through was rough, and I cannot begin to relate to what you are saying.* At least that response sounds sincere.

A year consists of 365 days, 366 if it is a leap year. What would it feel like if, out of those days, you live three hundred of them in sheer terror? Walking around on eggshells, not knowing when your father—your supposed protector—is going to erupt into an abusive rage fueled by alcohol or wickedness to attack you mentally, verbally, or physically and those around you?

These rages could stem from a plethora of things: why you are not walking fast enough when he calls you, why you forgot to answer with "yes, sir" rather than Dad or Daddy, why you are not eating your food the way he feels you should (i.e., fast enough), why he thinks you think like your mother's side of the family (i.e., stupid), why you and everyone else in the house is stupid, why you didn't bring his car keys when he asked for coffee, why you can't get more than a C average in math, why you cannot stay awake during a five-hour drive to Salisbury in the middle of the night and why you need to go to the bathroom during that five-hour drive, why you are two minutes late coming home from school after he timed the route and knows exactly what time you should be walking in the door, why his Whopper from Burger King is not hot after a twenty-minute drive and has cheese on it that he did not request, why you took longer to get another when he sent you back so he lost his appetite, or why your mother's mother keeps calling to check on her daughter and grandchildren since we were not allowed to telephone her.

I do not know why he was so paranoid, always listening on the other end of the phone line to make sure we did not inform Mom Mom Hamilton of the living conditions in the "King's Castle."

If he was not going into a tirade about those things, there were other ridiculous things that he verbally or physically attacked us for: why our mother had to go to the grocery store once a week and buy so many groceries when she couldn't cook anyway, why the groceries cost so much, why the groceries couldn't be brought into the house fast enough and not interrupt his game on television, why you left the door open, why you made so much noise folding the paper bags, why there were so many paper bags, why you fainted in temperatures over 100 degrees when he sent you to pick watermelons on his family farm at age ten without a hat, why you can't pump and carry two gallons of water to him fast enough without spilling any, why you can't run fast enough in every track meet to come in first place every time even though you participated in the National Junior Olympics for track and field every year from the age of thirteen and won 95 percent of the time.

The tirade might take another wicked turn. He would ask why Robert and I did not excel in everything like he did in school. Because of this lack, we would become nothings in society and get eaten up by the world. We got in trouble when the school bus was late, when it actually was him who was late the few times he dropped us off at Mrs. Spencer's house in the morning.

We could not do things fast enough. He would wonder why we were not shoveling three to five feet of snow fast enough and in the wrong direction, why our mother did not have dinner on the table when he arrived home, why she was five minutes late coming home, why she was stupid, why he had married her, why we needed a new pair of shoes every year since birth, why we needed new clothes when we had visibly grown out of the old ones, why we could not anticipate him needing more ice in his vodka, why we did not clear his plate as soon as it was empty, why we had to go to the doctor for an annual checkup when he thought nothing was wrong and doctors didn't know anything anyway, and that he could have become a doctor if he hadn't married your stupid mother, why you don't know which TV channel he wants to watch without him telling you, why we arrived home late from church services and why they don't finish sooner, why he cannot find our car in the church parking lot when he went to hunt us down, why he did not see our car on the road when we should have traveled the same route every time. At times he beat Mommy for not having traveled the same route every time since he mapped it out and always knew the right route to take.

He wondered why the ice cream he asked for was partially melted when we arrived home, why none of us could get anything right, and what a disgrace it was to live with such a pack of idiots. The list of whys went on and on and never stopped and had become a way of life.

I often wondered why my brother, mother, and I did not pour our troubles into an addiction like alcohol or drugs. Many people in our situation did, but I guess the Lord has the final say and had a plan for our lives that we could not see during those awful times. Crying out to the Lord was done in private. Mommy made this a part of her daily practice. She said things like *the Lord knows all about it, the Lord sees everything, God does not like ugly, the Lord looks out for fools and babies,* or *God's going to take care of it in His own way and time.*

We frequently overheard her crying in her bedroom with the door closed. When Robert or I tapped on their bedroom door to check on her, she always said she was all right, but we knew she wasn't. Mommy thought if she told us that she was all right, we would not worry as much. On the contrary—we worried every minute of the day. Her confirmations that the Lord would take care of us sounded good, but I wonder to this day why the Lord never took care of him. I wondered why the Lord did not take us out of that situation sooner.

For a long time, I was angry at God. I could not understand why He would allow those brutal beatings with two by fours on our backsides until we were too swollen to sit down, the beatings with leather belts when the metal belt buckles connected across our backs, the stomping and kicking when we were knocked down by his closed fists, the time he threw me through the front screen door onto the red brick porch, rendering me unconscious, for bringing home a C in math, the way he punched my brother in his asthmatic chest and taunted him to prove his manhood by striking back, punching Mommy with closed fists and throwing her to the hardwood floor and kicking her lifeless body, kicking and choking all of us, the hair grabbing and punching. What God would allow this to continue from when I was five to the age of eighteen? Who was this God?

As Christians, we are taught to rely on our faith to bring us through all things, especially troublesome and trying times. I remember as a child praying all the time that God would deliver my mother, brother, and me from the abusive turmoil. As a child, I never understood.

I tried to stay out of his sight, especially when he was drinking. I always did my chores, often doing extra ones that I was not asked to do to gain his approval. I tried to predict his every need. I did small things like place his slippers by his favorite chair in the family room so that when he arrived home from work, they were there. I helped Mommy prepare his plate and prepare his glass with the right amount of ice cubes. In school, I studied harder in my math classes but still was beat. As an adult, as I learned more about domestic violence through research and volunteer work, I learned that the abuser is responsible for his sinful behavior, not me.

Robert was a warrior and my hero. He stood back up whenever our father knocked him down. I wondered what Robert was thinking as our father stared him down, nose to nose, eye to eye. I think he thought he could intimidate Robert, but Robert always stood his ground. Mommy and I were not "Built Ford Tough" at all.

Why, when Mommy finally got up the courage to escape from him, would she be inflicted with cancer? When she finally had years of happiness ahead, why would He snatch those years from her and from us? Who was this God?

The Call

n the hotel room, the deafening ring of the telephone in the middle of the night pierced my soul. Toni, one of my closest confidantes, answered it. Her voice was whisper-soft so as to not wake me.

My eyes were closed, but I was awake. How could I sleep during a time like this? As she whispered, a chill ran through my body. A sinking feeling took over the pit of my stomach. I prayed the caller had reached the wrong room. As Toni quietly returned the handset to its base, she came over to my bed and whispered, "Wendy? Wendy? Are you awake?"

I did not answer. I had not slept since returning from Brandywine Memorial Hospital the day before, but she knew I was awake. She intuitively knew that I knew about the call.

Daybreak came quickly. We got showered and dressed and headed for the hospital. I had to see for myself. Aunt Gayle would be waiting for us in the lobby. Mommy would wake up for me.

We walked to the basement. Why was she in the basement? She hated basements. They were cold and damp with no soul. Whose idea was it to place her there? I would deal with them later. Right now, I had to see why Mommy was not awake.

We were led through two cold, metal doors painted institutional gray. As we pushed through them, a chemical odor I had never experienced before filled my lungs. Where was she? Where was Mommy? The only sound in the building was hollow, clicking footsteps on the cement floor.

Someone spoke. I did not know if it was Toni, Aunt Gayle, or the hospital worker. *Just lead me to my mother,* I thought. *She needs me.*

The final double set of gray doors swung open, and there she lay. She was sleeping peacefully on a stainless steel table. Her body was wrapped in sterile white bedsheets.

"Blankets! She needs blankets!" I protested.

Through the sheets, her body was cold to the touch. Her feet were freezing. Mommy hated her feet to be cold. "I asked for blankets, not sheets." I needed as many blankets as I could get. Until the worker returned, I lay my head on my mother's bosom and wrapped my arms around her to warm her body. What was taking that woman so damn long? It seemed as if she had been gone forever. Mommy was getting colder.

When she returned, I snatched the blankets from her. Quickly unfolding all three blankets, I wrapped each one around Mommy's cold body. I tucked the excess under her feet to trap the warmth. Wrapping my arms around her, I spoke her name repeatedly, begging her to prove them wrong. "Wake up, Mommy. Wake up. It's me, Wendy. Wake up. You can sleep later."

I saw the dryness in her nostrils, the dried debris that was evidence of the breathing tubes that had been removed. I made a mental note: *when she wakes, I will clean the area.*

Toni said she needed a cigarette and would be right back. "We'll be right outside, okay?" She and Aunt Gayle left.

"Take as much time as you wish," the worker said. She followed them out the door, leaving me alone with Mommy. That was just it. My time had come to an end. I returned my head to my mother's bosom, wrapping my arms around her body, and silently wept.

MY MOTHER'S FUNERAL WAS A DAY I WOULD NOT WISH on my fiercest of enemies. I awoke in the hotel in an infant-like state of mind. My boyfriend, Alonzo, had to lean over me and gently help me to sit up in the bed. Once upright, he gently pulled back the sheets. The tears began to flow down my cheeks. How had this day come so soon? He carefully removed the white sheet and gently placed his right hand behind the center of my back. His left hand carefully guided my legs out of the bed. I could hear the water running in the shower.

The warm droplets were soothing to my body, but they could not touch my soul. Oh, how I wished this day would have been drastically different. Tears flowed down my face, blending with the droplets hitting my body. My fist met the wall, furiously banging as I cried out to and for my mother. In a zombie-like state, I let the water pelt my face like a heavy rainstorm. If only the rain could turn torrential and drown me.

Alonzo's words penetrated my empty being, but I could not respond, could not move as he carefully bathed my soulless body.

My mind reverted back to the sight of Mommy in the hospital morgue. My mommy's petite silhouette was wrapped coldly in white like a mummy, her silky, blemish-free, ebony face with its finely chiseled cheekbones escaping the sheets. Her perfectly braided hair lay flat in sections on her head.

"Wake up, Mommy, wake up," I had whispered in her ear. No response.

Alonzo carefully towel dried me from head to toe. If he was drying me off, what was this warm sensation streaming down my legs? I reached down and felt between my thighs. The sight of my blood-stained fingers caused me to shriek.

"Your period is on," he said. "Do you have anything?"

"I'm dying. I'm going to die just like Mommy," I shrieked.

"No, you're not. I will not let you. Now do you have anything?" he repeated in a soft, commanding voice.

I stood paralyzed, bleeding, unsure of what he was saying.

He removed his pants and underwear. He disappeared into the bathroom and then returned with a handful of white stuff. "Lean forward. I will support you. Lift your right leg."

I barely lifted my right leg. He firmly guided it into one of the openings in the underwear. "Good. Very good. Once more, lift your leg."

I barely lifted my left leg, and he guided it into the remaining hole. He placed the pile of white stuff in the crotch of the underwear and gently pulled it up to my waist. Although the fit was tight, it was comforting.

The back hooks to my bra were clasped. While he helped me to sit on the bed, my stockings were slid up my legs one at a time with an awkward precision. My neatly pressed, off-white skirt was pulled up. My arms were carefully worked into the sleeves of the matching suit jacket. Three-inch, off-white pumps were placed on my feet as they dangled off the side of the hotel bed. My hair was freed of pink foam rollers, and the curls were pulled gently toward my lifeless, tear-stained face.

I asked to drive the short way to Mom Mom Hamilton's house. It seemed like forever. Driving had always been therapeutic to me, and on this day, I needed it the most. I drove in silence, hoping the road would be endless. Turning into the dusty, country gravel driveway, I was greeted by my family members' cars, carefully parked on the grass in a row facing the side of the house. I pulled into a space and parked the rental car.

Alonzo calmly said, "Take a deep breath. I will be right here beside you. Get out only when you are ready."

My Uncle Joe's car was parked beside our rental car. Seeing him standing by my door with a deep look of compassion and sorrow on his face was heartbreaking. His look of bewildered empathy transformed into a forced half-smile in an attempt at comfort. He slowly opened the door with his left hand and extended his right. Although so close, his palm seemed far away. I reached for his hand and placed my left foot on the carefully manicured lawn, my heels slowly sinking in the grass. My insides gave way. I vomited.

I do not know how I ended up in Mom Mom's bathroom on my knees, grasping the underside of the commode. I remember removing my suit jacket and thrusting it behind me. I switched positions and smacked down on the seat as my insides gave way again. I lifted my eyes to meet Alonzo's. He sat on the edge of Mom Mom's sea-green bathtub, my suit jacket folded in half across his lap. I thought my legs would fail me as I began to rise.

"You're bleeding," he said.

I stood there and stared, the tears flowing faster than ever.

"Do you have something?"

I didn't know what he meant. Have something? I said, "I have lost everything. I have nothing. How can I have something?"

He rose and gently placed his hand on my shoulder, pressing me back down on the commode. "Do you have something in the car that I can get for you?"

"I just want to stay here," I said through the tears.

A muffled female voice came from the other side of the bathroom door. Alonzo cracked it just enough to whisper instructions. He closed the door and sat back on the tub's edge with his eyes on the floor.

Another soft knock. Through the slightly cracked opening, he was handed a square object. He closed the door and handed it to me. I took it from his hand and examined it, unsure of its purpose.

"Can you put it on?" he asked.

I did not have a clue. The Kotex fell from my hand onto the sea-green bath mat.

CHAPTER 26

Free at Last

Mommy's funeral was the second time that I rode in a limousine. As the procession began down the road, I noticed things for the first time as if through a stranger's eyes. I never knew Uncle Joe and Aunt Mildred's house was so small or even that it was a trailer. Did the road always wind slightly, ending with a sharp slump? This all seemed new to me. All these trees on this road, all this open farmland—why hadn't I noticed these before?

Shortly, we arrived in front of Laurel AME church. Was the church always this small? Somehow, I thought it was bigger.

Cars were double parked along the country road with barely enough room to pass in a single lane. The small lawn alongside the church was riddled with cars parked three rows deep. How in the world were all these people going to fit in this church? The procession came to a slow, agonizing halt between two orange traffic cones. The urge to vomit was wrestling in my stomach. My bowels felt like they were going to release upon standing. *Why me, God? Why me?*

"Take your time, sister." Mom Mom's sweet, soft voice cooed to me.

My head never felt this heavy, as though a ten-pound weight was holding it down. As I struggled to raise my head, the tears flowed down my cheeks, under my jaw line, and down my neck.

Robert's eyes never looked so sorrowful, empty, hollow, and bloodshot. He desperately tried to look at me as if he were protecting me from it all, trying to deny that he himself needed to be protected. He looked so fine and stately in his dress blues. His pants were sharply creased, and his milk-white gloves were pristine. His black shoes looked like polished mirrors. Mommy was so proud of her son, the Marine.

"Ready, sis?" He asked as the door to the limousine opened.

The warm sunshine cascaded onto my face, drying most of my tears. A man extended his hand to offer assistance. I grasped it firmly, trying to remember how to stand without falling. The short, brisk walk up the church steps seemed to last forever. As our family entered, the congregation slowly rose to their feet. The hollowness in my throat was unyielding. The emptiness in my soul would last till my last breath. This was surely someone else's life, and I was merely playing the starring role.

Place one foot slowly in front of the other. I had to keep repeating this to successfully get down the aisle. The front pews were vacant and waiting for us. I slid in between Mom Mom and Robert. On this day, I would gladly relinquish my seat to someone else's daughter.

I will come back, I promised God. Mommy had loved this small, country church. I figured that if I bargained with the Big Guy, I would return in forty or fifty years—Mommy would have lived the next half of her life happily with family and friends and would be ready to meet Him by that time. I would be better prepared to let her go.

To this day, I don't know what the pastor said. I am sure the message was filled with messages of hope, life, and death. I know many loving, kind words were read from letters of acknowledgment from New York to Alabama. Mommy was loved by all who encountered her warm, loving, joyful spirit, her beautiful smile, and her heart filled with love for her children, family, and friends. The many floral arrangements represented the heartfelt wishes from across the miles. My apartment had filled with cards and floral arrangements from friends.

Mom Mom's hand rested on my thigh for comfort. Every so often, I placed my hand over hers to feel some warmth beyond my inner cold, to make sure this moment was real, that I was not caught in a bad nightmare. This gut-wrenching moment was real. My soul begged, *When will this eternity be over?*

The casket lid was opened. The woman laying inside was strikingly similar to Mommy. Her professionally styled, permed hair was curled to perfection off her face to expose her flawless, ebony complexion and model's sculptured cheekbones. Her glasses were cupped to her side in her left hand. Her dangling pearl earrings lay in their place on her ears. A slight, peaceful smile graced her slim, oval face. Pink was one of her favorite colors, and the blush-pink dress I had picked out with Aunt Gayle's help was perfect. The soft, ruffled collar and sleeves were as feminine as she was.

The funeral director motioned toward our family. It was time to say goodbye to the woman in the beautiful, rich, satin-lined mahogany casket. I clenched my stuffed Garfield to my breastbone. Mommy loved the Garfield cartoon character. It was her favorite, and she had bought me the stuffed animal, but I gave it back to her so she could have Garfield with her when she was receiving chemo treatments at the Hospital of the University of Pennsylvania.

Mom Mom's soft but firm palm cupped my elbow, helping me to rise on my trembling legs. Robert was on the other side of me, his arm around my waist. As I got closer to the beautiful woman with the peaceful smile, she looked more and more like Mommy. I took one last step closer.

It was Mommy.

I stared at her and saw myself. Memories of good times I cherished flashed, but the abusive horrors that she endured at the hands of my father trumped the good memories. *I will never leave you children.* Her promise echoed in my psyche. She was gone, and in that moment, so was I. Cupping my palm around her small waist, I leaned over to place a gentle kiss on her lips. The coolness of the touch seemed warm. Garfield fell from my breast to hers.

Lifting my right leg, I prepared to join Mommy. Someone yanked on my waist from behind. It was Robert. As I was lifted off the edge of the casket, I cried from the depths of my soul, "I want my Mommy! I want my Mommy!"

Someone grabbed Garfield and placed him back in my arms as I was led to my seat, wailing uncontrollably. "I wanted to give Garfield to Mommy," I exclaimed, looking up into Mom Mom's bloodshot, tear-filled eyes.

"It's okay. Mommy wants you to take care of Garfield," she said through her tears. She wrapped her arm around my shoulder and pulled my head closer to rest on her bosom. As I closed my eyes, the tears flowed. I had failed in my quest to join Mommy.

The ride around the block to Mommy's gravesite was slow but quick. As I was assisted out of the limousine, I felt my knees wobble. Sitting on those cold, green, velvet-lined chairs, staring at Mommy's casket, was unnerving. The undertaker handed red carnations to me and the other family members to place on the casket. One by one, the immediate family members came forward.

I was blinded by a bottomless feeling of purgatory and unforgivable rage. *He killed her.* My psyche was irrational. Mentally, I had checked out. My mind collided with my sanity, and I sat numb to what I was experiencing. Each family member came by, carnation in hand, expressing their sorrow to Robert and me as they walked past.

I know they all mean well, but I wish they would just shut up, I screamed inside my soul.

The pastor motioned for the family members to lay the carnations on the casket, and the funeral director formed them into a cross as they were offered. It was a beautiful depiction of a young life unfairly cut short.

This was my last chance. Robert led me to the casket, and the family slowly stood as we went to place our carnations on it. Deep inside my empty soul, I knew I had to jump in the open hole that held her casket, but something held me back. A will to live. Anger that he had stolen everything from her. I would not let him steal it all from me.

After the last prayer, I fled to the limo as fast as I could. I wanted to be away from it all. There was nothing else left. My mother was gone. My soul was gutted. As I knew it, life had ended.

Time was what I craved the most. If only we had more time. Precious time had been lost from the abuse her husband caused us all. We were supposed to be living right now, enjoying one another. He did this to us. His philandering ways brought the cancer that consumed her body. He snatched away our time, our future memories, my namesake, and my soul.

The limousine arrived in Mom Mom's driveway. I got out and searched the crowd of cars for ours. I wanted to get far away from the pain and never look back.

Alonzo was my outlet. Alonzo and I dated for a while. He was one of two people I met when I initially settled in Philadelphia. I loved him with my whole being. He took the time to know my inner soul better than me, and he always took care of me. Mommy loved him for me. He knew when I had enough and found me.

"How is my best girl?" His warm arm around my waist and heartfelt smile took me in.

"She will be all right," Mom Mom said as she came alongside me and also put an arm around my waist.

"Want to go for a ride?" he asked, attempting to rescue my beaten soul.

I nodded.

"We will be back," he said quietly and respectfully to Mom Mom.

"Okay. There is food in the house. Take good care of her, Alonzo."

He drew me in tighter and closer to his grip.

"There are so many people looking at me. I don't know what to say."

"Just walk with your head down, and I will guide you. The car is not far away." He opened the door to the car to let me in, walked around the car, and slid into the driver's seat. "We will be gone shortly."

I kept my head down and closed my eyes. The tears began once again. Ten minutes into the drive, Alonzo broke the silence, warmly touching my hand. "I need to change out of this monkey suit."

We arrived at the hotel room. He guided me over to the bed. "Lovey, what can I get you?" He spoke in a whisper, his hand resting on my shoulder.

"I want my mommy."

Sleep did not come easily. I awoke what seemed like a few moments later. The room was dark except for the light coming from the bathroom. I carefully lifted his arm from around my waist and crawled out of the bed. In the bathroom, two empty cracker and cheese wrappers were on the sink. Two unopened ones were nearby, surrounded by some scattered change. He must have been hungry during the night. As my underwear dropped to the floor, I stared at it. Why had I been wearing men's underwear? Nothing made sense anymore.

"Can I come in?" The door slowly opened, and Alonzo stood in the light. "Like the underwear?" he said with a half-smile.

I looked up without speaking. When I got back into bed, he pulled the covers over my naked body. The familiar, loving warmth of his arms wrapping around me returned me to comfort and safety. I stared at the neatly hung Jones of New York suit across the room. I would never wear it again.

My eyes slowly closed as I felt the love of a good man around me.

Comfort.

Safety.

Life was going to go on whether I wanted it to or not.

Imagine a future.

I would never be who I was, so that loss had been mourned. What was the "in spite of" as opposed to the "because of"?

He crushed our spirits. We allowed him to determine our worth. We were under the tyranny of his control.

What is the way forward? As I think beyond myself and look to the light, I am inspired to operate from a place of hope and purpose as opposed to darkness and hate.

Forgiveness was never asked for. Forgiveness has come. None of us look like our past. We are our futures.

MY WORDS

There are times when I smile,
Times when I cry,
I think of your face,
And a tear escapes my eye.
You were my world,
My inspiration and my heart,
But then you were gone,
I fell apart.

You were my best friend,
My one true confidante,
And that's not all you were.
You were also my mom.

I never knew how I would navigate life without you,
But you would have wanted me to,
And if there's someone I want to make proud and happy,
That someone is you.

These are my words to you.

DOMESTIC VIOLENCE SUPPORT RESOURCES

National Domestic Violence Hotline
1-800-799-SAFE (7233)

National Child Abuse Hotline
1-800-4-A-CHILD (422-4453)

NYC Domestic Violence Hotline
1-800-621-HOPE (4673)

Philadelphia Domestic Violence Hotline
1-866-723-3014